COMMUNITY RELATIONS
AND RIOT PREVENTION

COMMUNITY RELATIONS
AND RIOT PREVENTION

By

RAYMOND M. MOMBOISSE

Riot Advisory Committee of the
President's Commission on Law Enforcement
Advisory Committee of the California
Peace Officers' Association
Deputy Attorney General of the State
of California

CHARLES C THOMAS • PUBLISHER
Springfield • Illinois • U.S.A.

Published and Distributed Throughout the World by
CHARLES C THOMAS • PUBLISHER
BANNERSTONE HOUSE
301-327 East Lawrence Avenue, Springfield, Illinois, U.S.A.
NATCHEZ PLANTATION HOUSE
735 North Atlantic Boulevard, Fort Lauderdale, Florida, U.S.A.

With THOMAS BOOKS *careful attention is given to all details of
manufacturing and design. It is the Publisher's desire to present books
that are satisfactory as to their physical qualities and artistic possibilities
and appropriate for their particular use.* THOMAS BOOKS *will be true
to those laws of quality that assure a good name and good will.*

•

Printed in the United States of America
W-2

To my very precious wife, Mary Jane,
and our sons, Michael, Steve, and Mark,
whose love inspires my everlasting hope that
we can achieve understanding and love between all men.

ACKNOWLEDGMENTS

IT WOULD BE IMPOSSIBLE to acknowledge herein all those who have aided in the preparation of this book. Over the last few years I have had the pleasure of working with literally hundreds of peace officers and representatives of minority groups. As a result of that close association I have developed the utmost admiration for these men and women who are struggling to maintain order while at the same time protecting the rights of all people to full equality and a fruitful, productive life.

There are several that must be singled out for their very special help. First and foremost, I owe a special debt of gratitude to my wife, Mary Jane, and my three sons, Michael, Steven and Mark, for their patience and understanding during the long months of work on this book. Next, my secretary, Pearl Mitchell, who is not only a great secretary, but a loyal and close friend, deserves my very special thanks. There are others who must also be thanked. They are Paul Hannigan of the Sacramento Police Department for his advice and constructive criticism, which was always tempered with encouragement; Arthur Desmangles, who has always been there to help when I needed him; Bob Tyler, who has taken a lead in stressing the importance of education and understanding; and David Kelly, a dedicated young attorney who has contributed much to this book and to the achievement of better police-community relations.

RAYMOND M. MOMBOISSE

CONTENTS

Contents

COMMUNITY RELATIONS
AND RIOT PREVENTION

Chapter 1

NEED FOR PREVENTIVE PROGRAM

T HERE IS ONLY one good way to handle a riot—prevent it! Anyone who has ever witnessed such a holocaust is convinced of the truth of that statement.

No statistics, stories, news reports, or pictures can possibly convey the terror that a mob creates. Unless one has seen a city torn, bleeding and in flames, he cannot understand what a riot is like. Once he has witnessed it, he is driven by the compelling conviction that it must never be allowed to happen again, that there is only one effective way to control a riot—prevent it!

The first step along this path is mental. It is the recognition of the need for prevention and the realization that riots can be prevented.

The most dangerous myth is that violence is inevitable when two groups are in conflict. This fantasy takes many forms. At times it is said that trying to prevent violence will only generate more awesome violence. Again it is argued that if one lets violence run its course, things will be settled—the vanquished will "stay in their place."

The glaring defect of the "let things run their course" philosophy is that in human relations the course which is invariably run is a spiral from a minor disturbance to greater and greater mass rioting. Rather than being crushed, the vanquished will usually withdraw, regroup and nurse the ugly scars and hatred generated by the riot until they are able to retaliate successfully. The physical clash does not remove the basic cause which originally generated the riot.

Once it is recognized that remedial action is possible, the next step is to look for the causes. Having ascertained them, the

3

following step is to make a well-organized effort to eliminate the basic causes of riot, to relieve the frustrations which can lead to a conflagration.

As we shall see, the eradication of many of the causes of riots is not, strictly speaking, the responsibility of the local police. However, as is painfully apparent, the failure to find solutions will cause problems which it is their responsibility to solve, for the causes of riot are also among the leading causes of crime. Further, although the causes may not be the strict responsibility of the peace officer, they are problems of the community to which he belongs. In that community the peace officer is looked to for leadership in solving not only criminal problems but all social problems. Thus the police officer, whether he likes it or not, must play a predominant role in finding solutions for the problems that cause riots.

There is also a very broad area in which law enforcement can and must take affirmative action. The keystone of any such program is the development of an efficient, respected law enforcement organization. That organization must have the understanding and confidence of the community and all of the divergent groups and various elements in society. To achieve that end, the police must enforce the law fairly and impartially. They must convince all the people that all citizens regardless of race, creed, or color are treated equally under the law. The police must recognize the insidious cancer of prejudice, must realize the consequences that flow from it and do all they can to uproot it. Any such approach demands the cooperation of every individual officer as it is essential that he give serious thought to what he can do individually. Riots *can* be prevented! Riots *must* be prevented!

Chapter 2

CAUSES OF RIOT

INTRODUCTION

$\mathbf{A}$ RIOT DOES NOT suddenly occur. It is like the small part of an iceberg that juts above the waterline. Some eight-ninths of the block floats beneath the ocean surface and offers a much greater hazard to shipping than the part that can be seen. The breaking of heads and store fronts, the beating and terrorizing of streetcar and bus passengers, the shooting of defenseless and inoffensive women and men, the burning of automobiles—the riot events themselves, whatever they might be—are merely symptoms. They are the head pains that are symptomatic of a dread disease. They are not the disease itself. They are what shock you as you see them from the surface, but the worst part lies underneath.

The prevalent view about race riots, in more than one sector of our society, is that they are pathological, senseless and without meaning. This view, though widely held, is in error, for it fails to look beneath the surface of events to the deplorable living conditions, the social unrest, the sheer desperation that characterize the lives of the participants in these riots.

A riot is the culmination of tension that has been developing in the community over a long period of time. It is part of something much bigger. It represents an explosion of feeling arising from a festering discontent that could find no other, more acceptable avenue of expression and communication.

The control of the mob alone does not alleviate the conditions which caused the riot; at the most, the violence will call public attention to the unwanted conditions. In the final analysis, the most effective method of preventing riot and mob situa-

5

tions is to eliminate conditions which could lead to friction and misunderstanding and ultimately to violence and lawlessness.

It would be impossible to catalog all of the possible causes of riot or to set forth all of the danger signs. They will vary with time and place. We will attempt to point out only certain of the more important ones.

WEATHER

History indicates that there are certain times of the year when riots are most likely to occur. It is during hot, dry months that there is a greater possibility for the occurrence of riots and unlawful assemblies. Some of the reasons are as follows:

1. An increase in daylight hours, and daylight saving time.
2. Increase in leisure time during daylight hours.
3. Higher temperatures, causing people to spend more time out of doors (at the beach, parks and recreation centers).
4. Vacation and holiday time for more people.
5. Greater frequency in people-to-people contacts.
6. Opportunity for friction between people occurs more often.
7. Abbreviated clothing, leading to lowered inhibitions and arousal of sensual desires and passions.
8. Heat and humidity, causing a lower "kindling point" for tempers.
9. Increased sales and consumption of alcoholic beverages.

Obviously riots also occur during the colder months, particularly during vacation and holiday seasons. Labor-management disputes, which are of personal concern to large groups of people, and political disputes, also involving many people, can occur at any time of the year, but generally speaking, these flare-ups require a longer-lasting spark and are more easily extinguished by law enforcement personnel.

FRUSTRATION OF DRIVES, EMOTIONS AND GOALS

All human beings have drives, emotions and goals. Any unjust denial, actual or imagined, of man's basic rights, needs or aspirations will give rise to a feeling of frustration and desperation. In turn, frustration breeds aggression. Thus, outbreaks are most likely to occur where frustrations exist and where a community does not have an adequate institution for the peaceful solution of the problem, or when such an institution or committee is dormant or malfunctioning.

Either an exceedingly strong repression of the most important instincts, or a repression of a great number of them, is indispensable to produce an outburst. Further, it is necessary that the repression should spread over a considerable part of society. The repression of a small part of society exists everywhere; it leads to individual breaches of order which are called crimes. When the repression becomes general, it leads to a general breach and subversion of order.

Repression is, as everything else in the world, a relative conception. The poverty or the wealth of a man is measured not by what he has at present, but by what he used to have before, or by what the others have. The same must be said of the increase or decrease of repression. It increases not only when the difficulties in the way of satisfying the instincts grow, but also when they decrease at a different pace with various persons and groups. A man who sees a luxurious apartment feels badly housed atlhough he has for all purposes a satisfactory house. A man whose volume of rights is sufficiently large feels repressed when he is faced with the still greater privileges of other people.

Further, the festering frustration can (1) be exploited by elements of a community which are prone toward violence, and/or (2) serve as a foundation upon which additional grievance can build, all of which could lead to possible violent protest action. Because the repression of the main impulses will inevitaby force people to look for some way out, just as does the organism which is put into unfit surroundings, it is essential that we recognize and understand the basic human needs.

Human Needs

Individual or human needs may be separated into two different categories: physiological needs and social needs.

PHYSIOLOGICAL NEEDS. Basic physiological needs of the human

race include requirements for food, clothing and shelter. Without these necessities human life perishes. This brings into play
man's basic instinct for self-preservation and causes him to
take whatever action is necessary for his survival. Thus, history
reveals that time and time again civil disorders have occurred
when deprivation of these necessities became intolerable.

SOCIAL NEEDS. The following are accepted as social needs of
men: (1) security; (2) social approval; (3) recognition, and
(4) group association.

1. *Security.* The individual needs security both from the
elements of nature and from fear. Of these threats, the tangible
physical threats are easily recognized and the countering protective measures apparent. The same is not true of fear. While
real causes frequently exist, fears can and often do develop
from imaginary causes and will influence the actions of individuals as well as entire communities. These submerged psychological causes are more difficult to counter because of their
intangible phantom character. For this reason, the police must
be constantly alert to the temper of the community and any
changes that are indicative of fear.

Certain general principles will aid in this quest. The first
is the recognition that more and more in our present-day society
individuals look to their governments for security. Where such
governments do not or cannot provide for this need, individual
frustration will result. The feeling of frustration can lead to
an individual's participating in a civil disorder. Similarly the
breakdown of respect for the police, who are the symbol of
law and order, indeed of government itself will in turn cause
a weakening of the individual's security and sense of security.
By the same token, the failure of the police to protect society
will cause the deterioration of its sense of security.

Any society in the world exerts pressure on its members
and thereby affects their environment in one of two ways:
favorably or unfavorably. Thus a change in the environment
of an individual can result in a change of behavior. It is for
this reason that a people's sense of security may be jeopardized
when they are forced to accept the presence of an "outside"
group. Such an "outside" group would be identified as such if

it differed from the people in any of the following ways: racial composition, political ideology, religious beliefs and social standards.

2. *Social Approval.* The desire for social approval is one of the strongest urges of man. Children are taught to cooperate with and respect other members of their society. They are taught the customs and traditions to which their society adheres. Normally, individuals who violate the customs and traditions of their society face the imposition of physical harm, material harm, or social ostracism. The frustration of this drive for approval has time and again led to delinquency, crime and disorder.

3. *Recognition.* Regardless of custom or traditions, individuals and societies the world over compete for recognition. Recognition is a psychological factor indicative of successful living which lends prestige to existence. The recognition sought varies as to degree. It may be as simple as the need for respect and admiration of loved ones or as complex as the desire for recognition by a nation. Most men and nations will work long and hard to achieve recognition. If it is not obtained at least to some degree, men and nations may become frustrated and react.

4. *Group Association.* A man will seldom follow a course of action that will incur the disfavor of the group. He associates himself with a group and its objectives. Should a man be expelled from his group as an undesirable, he will in time seek association with another group. An individual who fails to attain a satisfactory degree of identification with one group is more vulnerable to the influence of other groups. The person who is, or feels himself, outside the mainstream of life will seek security in association or identification with extremism and will oppose society, indeed will foster its destruction.

Many countries in today's world are experiencing a massive and revolutionary upheavel which can be interpreted as basically amounting to a sharp cleavage of the present from the past. The objective being sought is a better life here and now as compared to the previous aim of seeking only a better life for succeeding generations. Through the progress of modern technology, the time-distance problem that once hampered the intercourse of people has been reduced. Modern news and communication media flash reports throughout most of the world in minutes. People are increasingly familiar with their neighbors and their inherent similarities and differences. Awareness of these surroundings has made the world seem a smaller place. With this awareness has come the desire for a better life. This reaction is natural and can be expected to continue. The rising tide of human expectations is attributed to individual and collective aspirations for the following: (1) independence; (2) justice; (3) wealth; (4) recognition; (5) self-esteem.

1. *Independence.* Through awareness, people have developed the aspiration for independence from subordination. They are no longer satisfied to endure unnecessary restraints upon individual sovereignty. They aspire to choose their own objectives. The aspiration for equality of opportunity and right of personal selection may be expressed by individuals or societies in various ways. They may attempt peaceful approaches to accomplish their goals; however, once motivated and organized, they will move by any means to attain their objectives.

2. *Justice.* Men aspire for equal administration of justice. They do not desire to be subjected to police brutality, unregulated search or seizure, or arrest without charges. Instead, they aspire to the right of equality before law for all members of society. Justice for the individual plays an important part in the rising tide of human expectations.

3. *Wealth.* The word *wealth* varies from society to society in its meaning and implications. An individual may be considered wealthy if he owns vast pieces of land; if he has a substantial sum of money; if he holds a prominent place in society; or if he possesses a large store of produce. Societies throughout the world use wealth as a measure of both individual and social progress. Men sense that wealth tends to add to their security regardless of their particular environment. With increased awareness of needs, they are becoming dissatisfied with the presumption that wealth can never be acquired. The aspiration for wealth is closely correlated with the individual's desire to obtain personal, economic and social privileges.

4. *Equality.* Men throughout the world are seeking to com-

municate their needs, problems and desires to their governments. Men are seeking the right to reason—to express themselves to other members of society. They are becoming dissatisfied with the role of subordinates who cannot assert themselves. In many instances, people are seeking to participate in their own government. They desire the right to arbitrate differences with their peers and their society. Some people have become aware that members of other societies in the world have attained this right; consequently, they are aspiring to attain the same goal.

5. *Self-esteem.* The aspiration for self-esteem is applicable both to individuals and to societies. It is closely correlated with men's desire for the right to independence, justice, wealth and recognition. Individuals want to be respected and considered equal to others of their society in their rights and privileges. Similarly, many formerly subordinated societies throughout the world are beginning to seek the same achievement. A group which has developed self-esteem will assert itself as it moves toward a predetermined goal. Self-esteem is a portion of the whole concept referred to as the rising tide of human expectation, which must be recognized.

SENSITIVE PROBLEM AREAS

In evaluating the tension derived from the frustration of human drives, certain specific sensitive areas have been referred to in the report of recent riots. They are as follows: (1) employment; (2) housing; (3) education; (4) merchant-consumer relations; (5) police-minority relations; (6) minority discrimination.

Unquestionably, minority discrimination constitutes a frustration of such magnitude that it generates tremendous tension. Certainly in recent years it has been the real or imagined cause that has run through most of our great riots. Certainly it cuts across, and at times is the root of, the other frustrations such as lack of jobs, improper education and inadequate housing.

Employment is significant because a man's job is a critically important indicator of his status in the community, as well as of his self-image as an independent, self-sustaining man. The absence of a job not only robs him of physical comforts, of housing and food, but, equally important, it robs him of an emotional, psychological sense of well-being and acceptance. The individual's self-image and sense of self-worth is greatly influenced by what he seems to be worth in the market of employment. Most of us have a tendency to become hysterical in our thinking when our jobs are threatened. Unemployment is a dreadful threat. When it stalks the land, the heedless do awful things to their fellow men in their mad scramble to preserve a little security. They claw and kick. They become Jew- and Catholic-baiters, Negro- and Nisei-haters. Whenever large scale unemployment prevails, people may become bitter, resentful and often desperate for the essentials of life, and are more easily led to riotous or unlawful actions.

In slum areas, overcrowding, substandard housing, unemployment and poverty-level incomes are often conducive to family breakdown and eventual social disorder. Most Negro ghettos are primarily matriarchal; many women are the main wage-earners and heads of families. Such family backgrounds help to explain—as a number of psychiatrists have observed—the inadequate role played by the man and father of the family.

Teen-agers growing up in such disturbed environments are further hampered in the search for identity, normal to all of them, by the absence of community resources that might aid in this search. Scholars studying crime in the urban community recognize increasingly that juvenile gang warfare and individual acts of violence may reflect not only individual pathology but also the absence of effective community life and meaningful bonds of social cohesion.

In recent years more and more attention has been directed to the importance of education. Any discrimination in this field will affect the potential employment potential of an individual and thus may generate friction.

Recent riots reflect a new cause—poor merchant-consumer relations. Poor and, in many instances, illiterate Negroes were often victimized by "lay-away" offers. A great source of friction lies in the repossessing of appliances and other items from financially disabled buyers unable to meet the required payments and other "added" fees. Often as much as 50 to 60 per cent of the total cost are lost in such repossessions.

The hostile relations claimed to exist between the police and the community are of particular concern, for in the last few years charges of police brutality have been bantered about more and more. The instances where such charges have proven justified have been infinitesimal. On the other hand, the times when the charges were deliberately made, as a part of a plan to harass and embarrass the police and to weaken law enforcement, have increased at a shocking rate.

RACIAL AND RELIGIOUS FRICTION

Although referred to in various ways in the preceding paragraphs, special emphasis must here be given to one of the great causes of riots, friction between racial, social, political or religious groups. The causes of that friction will be fully explored in subsequent material which develops the problem of prejudice.

INFLUENCE OR PRESSURE FROM AN OPPOSING IDEOLOGY

Still another factor causing civil disorders is the pressure or influence that may be caused by opposing ideologies, foreign or domestic.

Since the earliest beginnings of civilized man, history has recorded one ideology pitted against another. However, competition between ideologies does not always result in armed conflict. The police official must understand that an opposing ideology can use subtle and outwardly peaceful means to influence the behavior of his society. Civil disorders have become important tools by which governments are weakened, international relations jeopardized, and thousands of people injured or killed. There is every likelihood that these motivated civil disorders will continue to occur throughout the world just as they are occurring at the present time. A detailed discussion of the techniques utilized by such professional will be found in *Riots, Revolts and Insurrections.*

GOVERNMENT WEAKNESS

One element that is often ignored when considering possible causes for riots is the nature of the government itself. The failure of social institutions to function adequately or their inadequacy to resolve grievances will enhance the discontest of the members of society and greatly weaken their faith in that social order.

The effectiveness of the police is a key factor. Their impotence in dealing with disorder encourages more widespread and more lawless activity. When certain elements of society learn that they can successfully oppose the police, mob action is inevitable. On the other hand, when the police convince the public that law and order can be and will be maintained, the possibility of mob action is greatly decreased.

The public condoning, indeed encouragement, of the use of illegal methods of protest by high government officials and citizens who are held in high public esteem, has borne and will always bear bitter fruits of disorder. Those who riot do not draw, indeed are incapable of drawing, the sophisticated but sophistic distinction between illegal but peaceful flaunting of the law and an illegal and violent crime. Rather, the mob relies on the basic dogma of these leaders which, stripped of all its fancy verbal camouflage, is "The end justifies the means." Those in power who sanction violence of any type or degree encourage and nourish the mob, and ensure that there will be riot and revolt.

Thus, although eradication of many of the causes of riots is beyond the power of the police, they can do much to develop the confidence and respect of the people. This will in turn not only aid them in spotting any danger, but in preparing to cope with it effectively. Over and above that, the police can exert their considerable influence on the community to aid in the solution of many of the basic problems. They can by their example help to remove the blight of prejudice with all its fruits. They can forge the various minorities into one people.

Chapter 3

PREJUDICE

INTRODUCTION

For a police officer, learning techniques of dealing with problems of human relations, without also having some understanding of these problems, would be like learning to shoot a pistol without learning the particular situations in which to restrain from pulling the trigger. In human relations problems, as in handling his gun, the officer who acts without understanding can jeopardize the reputation of the whole force. Thus the officer must understand the nature and character of this thing we call prejudice, for human beings are not completely reasonable creatures. Fears and desires, some of them never even recognized consciously, influence a person's thoughts and acts. Early environmental teachings give direction to our life pattern, later experiences tend to reinforce these patterns, and because it is easier to believe than to think, it is only human to substitute prejudice for thinking.

DEFINITIONS

Prejudice is the bastard child of fear and ignorance. In general, the more intelligent, experienced, and educated a person is, the fewer prejudices he will have. The intelligent person thinks in terms of individuals; the ignorant thinks of groups.

As we shall see, prejudice is based upon ignorance, fear, superstition, selfishness, the tendency to shift the blame and other human weaknesses. It has no foundation in scientific fact. Nor is there religious doctrine or constitutional law which would serve as a basis for the belief that there is anything but a superficial and skin-deep difference between ethnic groups in our society.

15

The word "prejudice" is derived from the Latin *praejudicium*, meaning a legal procedure used in Rome to establish the social status of a litigant before trial; thus the world also meant a judgment made before the facts of a case were known.

Literally, it means *a prejudgment*—an opinion or leaning adverse to anything without just grounds or before the facts are established. However, literal translations of both Greek and Latin words sometimes are misleading. Prejudice is hardly a judgment, for a judgment is an operation of the mind which involves comparison, examination of facts, logical processes and good sense. Prejudice consists more of emotion, feeling and bias than it does of judgment. According to Webster's dictionary, prejudice is "an opinion or leaning adverse to anything without just grounds or before sufficient knowledge."

Perhaps the briefest of all definitions of prejudice is thinking ill of others without sufficient warrant. This crisp phrasing contains the two essential ingredients of all definitions—reference to unfounded judgment and to a feeling-tone. It is, however, too brief for complete clarity.

In the first place, it refers only to negative prejudice. People may be prejudiced in favor of others; they may think well of them without sufficient warrant. The wording offered by the *New English Dictionary* recognizes positive as well as negative prejudice:

> A feeling, favorable or unfavorable, toward a person or thing, prior to, or not based on, actual experience.

While it is important to bear in mind that biases may be pro as well as con, it is nonetheless true that ethnic prejudice is mostly negative. Indeed, because prejudice ordinarily manifests itself in dealing with individual members of rejected groups, prejudice has been defined as a hostile attitude toward a person who belongs to a group, simply because he belongs to that group, and is therefore presumed to have the objectionable qualities ascribed to the group.

This definition stresses the fact that while ethnic prejudice in daily life is ordinarily a matter of dealing with individual people, it also entails an unwarranted idea concerning a group as a whole.

Racial Prejudice

What is racial prejudice? Racial prejudice refers to those attitudes or beliefs concerning any minority, racial, ethnic, or national group that are disadvantageous to the members of that group. The term *racial* is used in its popular, not its scientific meaning. Hence, groups such as Negroes, Jews, Mexicans, or Irish, will be referred to as racial groups.

CATEGORIES

Prejudice may be broken into three general categories as follows:

1. Harmless—tastes in food, style of clothing, automobile makes, etc. These will do no harm except perhaps to your pocketbook or waistline.
2. Helpful—preference for one or another political party or public figure. These are not only desirable, but necessary in a dynamic republic like ours. We thrive on differences of opinion.
3. Hurtful—prejudices of an ethnic or religious nature. These involve bigotry, acts of discrimination, the false theory of the "second-class citizen," stereotypes and other like attitudes totally out of consonance with the American ideal of equality and fair play.

PREJUDGING

The essence of prejudice is that we are often disposed to prejudge, to pass judgment before we know the facts. Racial prejudice represents such a judgment regarding the inferiority of some groups and the superiority of others. Under the logic of race prejudice, any member of a group which is alleged to be naturally superior is, therefore, superior to any member of a group which is adjudged to be racially inferior. Thus, according to Hitler any "Aryan" German was superior to any and al of the French, the Czechs, the Poles, the Russians and t

Americans. The racially prejudiced individual claims that he is better than the members of other races. For example, those who profess the doctrine of "white supremacy" are saying, "I refuse to permit comparison between myself and any Negro, no matter what his attainments. I am superior because of my birth. I was born that way."

It is thus apparent that having a prejudice involves several things. For one, the prejudiced person believes certain things about whole groups of people. These beliefs are usually based on insufficient or incorrect information, but the prejudiced person holds to these beliefs as if they were facts. For another thing, the prejudiced person feels certain things about whole groups of people. Fear, hostility, anger and other negative emotions are directed against the objects of prejudice.

Individual members of the groups against which prejudice is directed are thought to have all the negative qualities attributed to the group. The prejudiced person does not think of them as individuals, with attributes quite different from those of all other individuals. He thinks of them in terms of a stereotype, a sort of composite of all the qualities attributed to the group. The prejudiced person who meets a member of the group against which he is prejudiced thinks he knows all about the group member, even before he has actually had an opportunity to speak to him, hear about him, or work with him.

There is another aspect of prejudice which is rather interesting; that is, that prejudiced people are rarely prejudiced inst one group only. Usually, prejudice is indicative of a 'e approach to life, and the prejudiced person is suspicious arful of other groups, new ideas, and almost everything is different or strange to him. Fear and hostility are in him than are curiosity and interest, so he has a to reject without investigating, to condemn in spite

DISCRIMINATION

n is an act of total or partial exclusion prompted nerally, this exclusion is not based on the individual's personal worth, but on a label branding him as a member of a discredited group.

Discrimination is the acting out of the beliefs and feelings of prejudice. Discrimination means restricting members of minority groups to separate facilities of all kinds, such as places of amusement, restaurants and schools. It means employing them in menial jobs only, regardless of their ability to do other kinds of work. It means treating them as inferiors, generally, and as undesirables. It means subjecting them to many deprivations and having their ambitions and desires constantly frustrated.

BASIS OF PREJUDICE

There are a great many explanations of how prejudice began, and just how it is perpetuated in our culture. Historical, social and psychological reasons all contribute to a complete understanding of the phenomenon of prejudice. No one explanation is sufficient to cover all the causes of prejudice.

To understand why a person is racially prejudiced involves the understanding of the individual's needs, the demands that are satisfied by his negative beliefs and attitudes, and how racial prejudice serves the person in the solution of his personal problems.

Pathological Personality

Not all racially prejudiced people are mentally sick nor are all mentally sick people racially prejudiced, but the individual with a pathological personality sometimes manifests racially prejudiced attitudes in order to support his deviant behavior.

Free-floating anxiety is based on the existence of tensions, having no reference to a particular or specific object. The tensions are reduced through attacks on others. Ultimately, an individual may learn to direct his aggressive behavior against a specific group.

The paranoiac is usually a very suspicious person, a person suffering from delusions. A paranoiac may fix his suspicions on members of a minority group to justify his behavior.

Although the number of people whose overt prejudice is attributable to paranoia or free-floating anxiety is insignificant, these people nevertheless may exert a strong influence on others. Often these people are found as leaders of antiracial mobs, organizations and ideologies.

Prejudiced Personalities

There are some people whose whole personality is structured in such a way that prejudice remains vital to them—unless they get prolonged and expert help. These people all show similarities in behavior, traits which are closely related to prejudice. For example, they have a tendency to idealize their parents, attributing to them only qualities of goodness and purity and excellence. They find it impossible to view their parents as human beings, with faults as well as virtues. This is a kind of stereotyped thinking which is similar to thinking about minority groups in terms of stereotypes. Although they are quick to say they like their parents, psychological examination usually reveals that they feel much antagonism toward their parents, which they are unable to express.

Similarly, these "prejudiced personalities" are usually extremely moralistic, that is, they make much of the conventions, and are very harsh in judging the moral transgressions of others. They find it difficult to allow for human weakness, to be compassionate and understanding. Things are either right or wrong, people are either good or bad. There is no room for compromise, for tolerance, for the realization that the same person may be both good and bad, strong and weak, honest and dishonest, depending upon what he has learned, what the circumstances are, and what he believes and feels in a specific situation.

They apply these same standards to themselves, and because they cannot fail to see that they are sometimes good and sometimes bad, sometimes loving and sometimes hostile, they cannot accept themselves as worthy individuals. Here again, by perceiving whole minority groups as less worthy than they are themselves, they are able to go on living.

Such people, generally, cannot be changed in ordinary teaching situations. However, interestingly enough, because of their deep-seated insecurity and great need to be accepted by others, they will often go along and, generally accept minority group people if they see others in their own group behaving in a tolerant and accepting manner. They will behave in the same way even though their attitudes will not undergo much change.

The man who searches his own heart occasionally in prayer knows that he, himself, reflects the glory and the beauty and the variety of God in many things which he does. Such a man does not find it difficult to recognize every other human being as a fellow reflection of God's wonders. He instinctively demands for this fellow creature all that he sees as necessary for dignified human life.

For racial hatred to take root in a society and spread, strict notions of morality must be gradually weakened in the minds and hearts of the members of that society. A man must first justify to himself his desertion of his fellowman. Only when the restraints imposed by morality are completely gone can prejudice flourish without opposition. From there on, the only rule which will matter in life can be summarized briefly: "Dog eat dog."

Frustration and Hatred

Tensions arising out of the frustration of almost any significant need often find expression in aggressive acts which seem to allay temporarily the frustrated state. Indeed it has been said that aggression serves an escapist function and has a drug-like capacity to soften the disappointments and frustrations of life.

Because anger is a transitory emotional state, aroused at a given time by an identifiable stimulus, the tendency is to attack the source of the frustration directly and to inflict injury upon this source.

Anger differs from hatred in that anger is customarily felt toward individuals only, whereas hatred may be felt toward whole classes of people. A person who gives way to anger is often sorry for his outburst and pities the object of his attack, but in expressing hatred, repentance seldom follows. Hatred is more deep-rooted, and constantly desires the destruction of the object of hate.

To put the matter another way, anger is an emotion, whereas hatred is a sentiment—an enduring organization of aggressive impulses toward a person or toward a class of persons. Since it is composed of habitual bitter feeling and accusatory thought, it constitutes a stubborn struction in the mental-emotional life of the individual. By its very nature hatred is extropunitive, which means that the hater is sure that the fault lies in the object of his hate. So long as he believes this he will not feel guilty for his uncharitable state of mind.

There is a good reason why out-groups are often chosen as the object of hate and aggression rather than individuals. One human being is, after all, pretty much like another—like oneself. One can scarcely help but sympathize with the victim. To attack him would be to arouse some pain in ourselves. Our own "body image" would be involved, for his body is like our own body, but there is no body image of a group. It is more abstract, more impersonal. It is especially so if there is some visibly distinguishing characteristic. A different-colored skin removes the person to some extent from our own circle. We are less likely to consider him an individual, and more likely to think of him only as an out-group member. But even so, he remains at least partially like ourselves.

There is another reason why it is easier to hate groups than individuals. We do not need to test our unfavorable stereotype of a group against reality. In fact, we can hold it all the more easily if we make "exceptions" for the individual members we know.

This basis for racial prejudice is applicable only to a small segment of those who are racially prejudiced. Many people who are under great tension are not aggressive toward members of minority groups. There are a number of tension-reduction techniques aside from hostility toward minority groups. Additionally, it is impossible to show that all people who are racially prejudiced have suffered more frustrations than people who are not racially prejudiced.

Repressed Tensions

Tensions which are in conflict with one's moral ideology are often repressed. One possible effect of such repression is projection, that is, attributing to others one's personal shortcomings. When the projection is applied to a whole race of people, we have another example of racial prejudice.

Ignorance

Generally it can be said that prejudices are based on ignorance and superstition. We fear and make up stories about things and people we do not know. Ignorance of the next man's ways, his culture, his beliefs, forces us to fill the gaps between our knowledge with absurd theories. The more you know about the man, the better you will understand his ways and the more tolerant will you be of him.

Psychologists agree that prejudice is 100 per cent learned. While we are not born with hate, we do possess the ability to develop hate. What and whom we learn to hate will depend largely on our experiences at home, in our neighborhood and in our schools, and the impressions these experiences make on us. No one inherits his prejudices. A child may be told by his mother that if he doesn't behave, she will send for a policeman who will put him in jail. Repeated often enough, the child acquires a fear of, and consequent prejudice against, all policemen. In the same way, children hear their parents and older associates talk about Negroes, Jews, Catholics, etc., and they acquire prejudiced ideas about these and other groups.

The home is the most important source of our opinions and beliefs. To a very young child his parents are persons to be imitated and followed. This is not difficult to understand when we take into consideration how dependent the child is on his parents for food, security, comfort, love and protection from danger. The attitudes of the parents become, in the mind of the child, associated with the food, love and protection, and he accepts them just as he accepts without question the creature comforts.

Parents also provide the child's main source of knowledge. He in a sense becomes a book, edited by his parents. If he is reared where racial prejudices are not present and where tolerance is the general attitude, then he does not develop racial

prejudice at this point. But if the home has an attitude of
intolerance and prejudice, then the probability is that the child
will also be intolerant and prejudiced.

It is sometimes difficult to accept as fact information which
seems to indicate that those things we believe and which our
friends and relatives believe are all wrong. No one likes to
admit that the basis for what he has been thinking and doing,
and teaching his children is a hodgepodge of falsehood, fear
and error. However, let us bear in mind that we learned to
believe and to feel long before we were capable of using
reason to evaluate what we were learning. When we were
children and we heard our parents speaking, we never stopped
to question the accuracy of what they were saying. We did
not consider their sources of information, nor did we wonder
about how their own fears and uncertainties influenced their
ideas. We listened to the beliefs of our parents and they became
our beliefs; what they feared and hated, we learned to fear and
hate; and what they accepted as truth, we believed.

However, human beings have an amazing facility for learning, changing and adapting to new conditions. As long as we
live, we can unlearn old ways and learn new ways in the light
of the new insights new skills, and new information we acquire.

Rationalization

Beliefs and attitudes of racial prejudice are developed in
many racially prejudiced people in an attempt to resolve so-
cially disapproved urges, such is impulses of cruelty, greed and
sexual aggression. A citizen must inhibit these urges because
society disapproves of such behaviors.

It is easy to see why many people who have negative
attitudes toward minority groups still do not think they are
prejudiced. To be prejudiced is to be unreasonable, and it is a
person of rare self-confidence and insight who admits that he
has been somewhat less than reasonable in his attitude or
behavior. Consequently, most prejudiced people pad their
prejudices with layers of rational explanations to save their
consciences from twinges of pain. These people can give dozens
of examples of minority-group members who deserve to be

discriminated against. They will demonstrate how almost every minority-group member they have met fits the stereotype which they hold of that group. If they are forced to concede that some individuals do not fit the stereotype, they will admit that these individuals are exceptions to the general rule, and that their existence merely proves the rule that most members of the minority group do conform to the stereotype. By the same token, when told that our stereotype image is in error, we are being told not only that a cherished belief is wrong, but that the people we love have taught us a lie. Naturally, we will reject the new information—and we will probably reject it with some show of anger.

There is an interesting thing about this mechanism of rationalization—of finding "reasons" to justify behavior and attitudes. The human organism has a tendency to see and hear and accept as fact only those occurrences which do not violate the beliefs and feelings it already holds. It selects from the environment those things which strengthen its preconceived ideas. Consequently, a person who believes that Jews are loud will actually find in his own experience that all Jews are loud. He will not meet or notice Jews who are not loud; he blocks such Jews out of his consciousness, so that he will not have to change his attitude toward Jews in general. If he believes that all Italians are emotional, he will interpret the gestures, facial expressions and choice of words of the Italians he meets as evidences of overemotionality. He will not believe that broad gestures and facial mobility are characteristics of many national groups, and that there is no evidence that people who behave in this way are more emotional than are people whose movements are smaller and less facile.

The point is that all of us can fall into the trap of rationalization if we are not continually on guard. And that guard means that we must know the facts, and develop skill in the step-by-step process from facts to conclusions. In some matters, as we have said, this is not difficult to learn. In other matters, in which our emotions are involved, it is very difficult to learn to reason. We need first, the desire to learn, second, expert help in learning, and third, a long period of time devoted to learning.

A lifetime is too short a time for most of us to be able to unlearn faulty reasoning in some areas of our activity.

Tabloid Thinking

Another reason is "tabloid thinking" or oversimplification of a situation. Strife brings out the helplessness with which the individual faces world-wide forces. He needs to simplify issues in order to make possible some understanding of social chaos. Oversimplification of issues saves energy. If a person feels hostile and aggressive, it is easier for him to attack one single obstacle in his path than to spread his aggressive impulses.

Generalizations

Many people form general opinions of groups based on their unfortunate experiences with a few members of the group. They do not think of people as individual persons, but rather, they place them in carelessly formed, all-embracing classifications. When a group is uniformly looked on in this manner, it is called a "stereotype." For example: "Irishmen are drunkards," "Negroes are lazy," "Jews are greedy," "Puerto Ricans are ignorant," "Italians are gangsters." This thinking is a distortion of normal reasoning. It stereotypes a whole group without regard for individual qualities.

Actually, factual justification for prejudice cannot be found in the traits of minority-group members. The man who tells of being cheated by a Jew, or attacked by a Negro, does not prove that all Jews are cheats or that all Negroes are violent. If he maintains that this proves anything about whole groups of people, he is overgeneralizing.

This becomes clearer if you are speaking of members of your own groups. For example, if you are dealing with the case of a white man who has held up and beaten a storekeeper, if you are Caucasian, you may think the crime a terrible thing. You will probably not think, "That crime is a reflection on my people, and on me." It is not likely, either, if you are a Negro, that you will think, "Isn't that just like a white man!"

However, if the criminal in this case is a Negro, many white people are inclined to think that this is typical of Negro behavior. Now, we know that the overwhelming majority of Negroes are peaceful, quiet, law-abiding people about whom we never hear. Yet many people use each case of a Negro lawbreaker as "proof" that Negroes as a group are criminals. This is overgeneralization.

Group Pressures

There is another reason why it is often not so easy to relinquish the prejudices learned as part of a way of life. Let us consider this example. An individual learns to appreciate the differences he observes in people. He learns to get along with all of them, work and play with them, and never think that there are any insuperable obstacles to their being friends. When he goes home, he finds that his family is disturbed because a minority-group family is moving in next door. He discovers that the teen-agers on the block are planning ways to harass the new family and force them to move. He sees that the whole climate of opinion and attitude in his social environment is different from the attitudes and opinions he has learned in school. Will he dare to protest that his family, that his friends in the neighborhood, that most of his world are wrong, and that he is right?

So it is with the adult. What a man is, he likes. What his group prefers, he prefers. What they reject, he rejects. His is the "in-group." An "out-group" is looked upon as inferior, and becomes the subject of hatred and resentment when it is thought to threaten the security of the "in-group." When Negroes or Puerto Ricans begin "invading" in large number, the "in-group" feels insecure.

Groups satisfy man's basic social needs for security, response, recognition and belonging. Group identification tends to enlarge personal horizons which may either reinforce or modify existing views and attitudes of group members. Being able to criticize enhances one's ego, and criticism is more easily voiced among like-minded people. Their assent reinforces a belief in the rightness of their views. Lack of opposing views leads to overrating the strength of their position.

Even if he begins to have misgivings about his attitudes

toward minority groups, he often feels impelled to continue to speak and act in the same way his friends and relations act. A person wants to be accepted by his group. He is not willing to alienate those who are important to him. It is easier to go along with what everybody is thinking, and keep your doubts to yourself—at least until there is some reason to believe that social support will be forthcoming if these doubts are expressed.

Scapegoating

Living conditions in the present world are extremely complex. The individual does not normally know enough about economics and political science to understand the reasons behind various economic and political maneuvers. Because he feels the necessity for establishing in his own mind the reasons why things are being done, he is inclined to oversimplify what he thinks. Instead of figuring things out, he secures a scapegoat for his misunderstanding.

Sometimes the issue may be simplified by blaming a group or class of people rather than a specified individual. For example, in Boston's Coconut Grove fire, the public blamed "the officials" rather than concentrating its wrath on any one person, against whom a more detailed, and therefore more difficult, bill of charges would have to be drawn.

Everyone has a natural desire to feel superior. Those who can satisfy this desire by being a better-than-average officer, a successful executive, a distinguished teacher, or other desirable achievement—that is, those people who are confident of themselves and their ability, who have a sense of worthwhileness about their lives and what they are doing—do not have to rely on feeling superior to other people. They do not need to feel that whole groups of people are inferior to them before they can think well of themselves. They do not need anyone to look down on.

On the other hand, the person who is not sure of his own worthiness, the one who is afraid of himself and life, who needs to bolster his ego which has been damaged by his past experiences of unresolved conflict or repeated failure, is the person to whom prejudice is important; for prejudice is largely based on insecurity and fear. Fear has been described as an actual feeling of danger and dread, which can be reduced or dispelled by an attack on that which we consider to be a threat. Frequently we do not distinguish properly between real and false threats, and strike out against things which actually pose no threat to us.

Anxiety is the anticipation of danger. Like fear, it is caused by a feeling of basic insecurity. It can sometimes be alleviated by ralionalization which may take the form of scapegoating.

One seeks a scapegoat to enhance his feelings of self-importance. A person who feels insecure can sometimes convince himself of his basic worth by increasing his feelings of strength. The bully who seeks to prove his strength by mistreatment of a physically weaker child is an example of this tendency. Conversely, a physically weaker child may attempt to affirm his strength by verbally scapegoating his stronger companions. He may then physically bully a still weaker child to compensate for his own feelings of inferiority. He can blame minority-group members for his failures and will be quick to see inferiority in a whole minority group of people because, by comparison, he will then feel superior.

Thus, he perceives the differences between groups as marks of inferiority or superiority rather than just interesting or unimportant differences. When he meets a man with dark skin, he will think, "This man is not as good as I am," and this feeling will often govern the behavior he demonstrates toward the Negro. In turn, he may expect deference and subordination, which will add to his feeling of superiority. If, in addition, he believes that this man, just because he is a Negro, is a less skillful worker, less ambitious, and generally less desirable as a human being, do you see what this can do for the person who needs to feel superior?

Very similar to this need to feel superior is the need to blame someone else for one's own feelings of inadequacy, for one's own shortcomings and failures. If the people blamed are members of a minority group in our society, he often gets social approval for blaming them. So, in addition to getting the burden of guilt off himself, in addition to having the pleasure of blaming someone else for his own limitations, he gets the sanction and approval of society for his behavior. So, the man who is prejudiced goes through life seeing only those traits and behaviors of minority-group members which tend to reinforce his prejudices. He carefully selects from in front of him only those traits which "prove" he was right all along. He either ignores those traits which indicate he is wrong, or else he reinterprets them so that they fit into his pattern of prejudiced thinking. To maintain his superiority, he fiercely resists any new knowledge which may make him doubt that his attitude and behavior toward minority groups are right.

We must emphasize a danger inherent in thinking that minority-group people are all inferior to majority group people. Prejudiced members of the majority group, who may have personality traits which are preventing them from realizing their full potential either professionally, economically, or personally, may be so blinded by their feelings of superiority to other groups that they will do nothing to help themselves. So, in the long run, they are less happy and less successful than they might be if they were not prejudiced.

These emotional barriers to changing attitudes and behavior show how difficult a job it is for the person who is convinced that prejudice and discrimination are undesirable to convince others in turn. Just telling people how wrong they are may often do more harm than good. The person who is told he is wrong may do everything he can to prove to himself that he is right beyond any doubt, and in the process he will so strengthen his conviction that it will make it even more difficult to change him.

Specification of a Scapegoat

Fear is not the only concomitant of prejudice. Often anger and hostility lie at the bottom of prejudice and discriminatory behavior. When people are prevented from doing the things they want to do, they are likely to react by hitting at something or trying to make someone else unhappy. Failure and other emotional disturbances must be released. When a person cannot hit back at the thing that makes him unhappy, he finds a substitute, a scapegoat. A suitable scapegoat should be highly visible with distinguishing, salient features, or recognizable through some trait of dress or behavior; available; already the object of latent hostility; a symbol of something loathed or despised; not strong enough to fight back. In this regard, it is interesting to note that segregation markedly enhances the visibility of a group. It makes it seem larger and more menacing than it is.

Obviously the minorities satisfy these specifications. Thus it is that people often seek to place the blame for the ills of society upon some group. Jews, Catholics, Negroes and Puerto Ricans make identifiable targets when trying to shift the blame for social inadequacies from oneself. In most cases, there is no foundation for the evil which is imputed to the victim. It is usually an unconscious attempt to "unload" one's own sense of inferiority and guilt. By blaming minority groups, we then get a twofold satisfaction; we absolve ourselves from the guilt of failing, and we get the approval of people we know because we are agreeing with their point of view.

Myth of Innate Differences

Another "reason" propounded to justify the belief that minority groups are inferior is that of "innate" differences. It is believed that people of a different racial stock inherit different natural capacities, and that the superior race must control the inferior. It is further assumed that biological amalgamation with the inferior race will cause the superior race to degenerate. Although this myth is usually thought of as being a belief unique to the white race, many other races—black, brown and yellow—have held to the same myth.

There are a great many things which may be, and have been, said about human nature. We will confine ourselves here to a discussion of human nature as it pertains to the problems of prejudice and discrimination. Most evidence points to the fact that what we are pleased to call human nature is the traits and skills we have learned by interacting on one another. Psychologists have learned that people everywhere have certain basic needs. These needs are learned while such biological drives as hunger, thirst and avoidance of discomfort are being satisfied. Thus, the child learns love and cooperation—and the need for love and cooperation—in those first days of his life when his mother is satisfying his hunger and changing his wet clothes.

People often make the mistake of attributing differences in human nature to people of different ethnic groups. If human nature is formed through the child's early relationship with his mother and, then, with other members of his family, what differences are there in these early relationships of the various ethnic groups which could possibly result in any drastic differences in human nature? There are, of course, individuals whose parents reject them, neglect them, and deny them the love they need to become cooperative and loving human beings. Yet, we find such individuals in all ethnic groups and all social classes.

Likewise, if it were "human nature" to fear Negroes, or hate whites, or hold Puerto Ricans in contempt, or laugh at differences in languages and customs, all of us would act in this way. If it were "human nature" to want to keep certain people in menial jobs, to want to keep them from enjoying certain public facilities, to want to prevent them from getting a decent education, then we would all want these things. Obviously this is not true. Rather, we have learned to think and act in these ways, and all around us we can see adults continuing to teach children to accept as natural these ways of thinking and acting.

Surely, conflict, too, is a part of that "human nature" which we have learned by interacting, but, conflict can be stimulating and productive of good. Conflict then becomes creative rather than destructive; it results in progress rather than loss of life and threats to civilized living.

Human nature, then, is what we choose to make it. It is the result of what we teach our children and how we treat them, and, since it never ceases to change, we can—even in adulthood successfully continue to change it for the better.

Historical Basis

Many of the prejudices can be traced to the "old country"

and back through the decades, and even the centuries, to ancient religious, national and racial conflicts between people of the "old world." Descendants of these people, emigrating to America, brought with them some of their stock prejudices against others, and settling down "among their own," retained them and passed them on to their children.

Competition and Conflict

Ours is a competitive society. Not only individuals but also nations and racial groups are in competition with one another as they strive individually and collectively to improve their economic and social status. It is almost inevitable that such competition for jobs, a place to live, access to higher social position, and the struggle for a generally higher plane of living will bring about some measure of conflict; and each in our separate ways will seek to retain whatever superior advantages we may already possess. It is out of this competition that conflict may arise, and the outsider, the newcomer, the stranger, is often stigmatized as inferior. Thus the theory that when groups compete, hostilities and prejudices often arise.

Economic reasons for antiminority prejudice run through the pattern of our country's development. On the West Coast, the Chinese people were accepted until they began to compete for jobs the Caucasians wanted. In the East, the Irish, the Poles, and other immigrant groups constituted sources of cheap labor as long as they could be kept disorganized and discriminated against. In the South, Negroes are a potential threat for poor whites if they are permitted to compete on an equal basis for jobs.

During bad times, generally, when unemployment and scarcity of goods and shelter create anxiety in many people about the future, there is a tendency among some to allay their anxiety by blaming a particular group of people for their misfortune. It is easier to blame someone you can see than it is to blame the combination of fearful and little-understood forces which really cause depression and poverty.

Exploitation Theory

Still another economic theory advanced is that prejudice is

useful to an exploiting class in maintaining economic privileges and to justify exploitation of either the group itself or its resources.

There is an inference in this theory that prejudice is a deliberate, well-studied plan to be used for a specific purpose. This is contrary to the larger volume of studies which indicate that prejudice is emotional in nature. Although there is little doubt that prejudice can be taught and that an exploiting class can do the teaching for their own purpose, once prejudice is learned it cannot be turned on and off like water from a faucet.

Demagogues and Special Interests

Our intensely competitive social and economic life is further complicated and aggravated by the presence among us of many disturbing elements. There are individuals and groups who have a deliberate interest in fanning the flames of nationalistic and racial hatreds. Often, as in the case of the Nazis in Germany, they are interested in setting up scapegoats among the various nationality and racial groups. By this means, they are able to divert attention from their own unquestionable purposes. The idea of racial superiority and inferiority has become a powerful and dangerous weapon. It is used by groups seeking to divide the population on economic questions. During political campaigns, this same device of "divide and conquer" has been used to direct the public's attention away from the real and basic issues. Unsupported charges hurled at a minority group may be decisive in a political campaign or a labor dispute. There are cunning and irresponsible leaders who are interested in intensifying racial, religious and nationalistic hatreds. In the chaotic situation which would ensue, they propose to make their bids for power. Only then do their venal and questionable objectives become readily apparent, but then it is often too late.

CONDITIONS THAT MAKE FOR PREJUDICE

The ten sociocultural conditions that seem to make for prejudice are the following:

1. Heterogeneity in the population.

2. Ease of vertical mobility.
3. Rapid social change.
4. Ignorance and barriers to communication.
5. The relative density of minority group population.
6. The existence of realistic rivalries and conflict.
7. Exploitation sustaining important interests in the community.
8. Sanctions given to aggressive scapegoating.
9. Legend and tradition that sustain hostility.
10. Unfavorable attitudes toward both assimilation and cultural pluralism.

CONSEQUENCES OF PREJUDICE

The consequences of prejudice are of serious concern to all of our people, for the bitter fruits of it affect us all. Prejudice in the community makes for disharmony and antagonism. People tend to withdraw into their shells, form pressure groups, seek to promote their own interests without regard to the welfare of society generally. In a word, prejudice and discrimination pit one group against another in an unhealthy competition out of consonance with democratic principles.

In a heterogeneous society such as our, with hundreds of thousands of Italians, Irish, Negroes, Jews, Germans, Puerto Ricans, etc., living and working in such close and, sometimes, trying circumstances these prejudices can be of momentous import, creating disunity and tension which, in turn, can lead to tragic conflict and civic shame.

For the holders of prejudice, prejudice limits and distorts an individual's point of view, closes the mind to facts, and makes unbiased judgment impossible. It stagnates the mind it occupies. Some people become possessed by their prejudices. They cannot think. They can only fear and hate. Such people are bigots. They are usually insecure, frustrated and ignorant individuals and they blame whole groups of people for whatever is wrong in the community, nation, or world.

The objects of prejudice are set apart from the general society and regarded as different, inferior, dangerous, or all three. Because of the prejudice and discrimination so frequently directed against them, members of minority groups are more than usually sensitive and defensive. This is not too difficult to understand, for when people are made to feel from childhood that they are different from other people, they are bound to be affected in some way.

Prejudice is contagious. Discrimination against any one group will quickly lead to discrimination against other groups. If any man passively tolerates vicious discrimination against any group, he moves the day close when he will be the victim of the same kind of discrimination himself. Though we don't reflect on it often, every man is necessarily a member of several minorities (religious, racial, social, professional, cultural).

Prejudice is bad for business. Those areas of the country which have been cursed with violent racial conflicts resulting from prejudice have become bitterly aware of the price tag that it attached to racial hatred. A business firm cannot be blamed for not wanting to move into an area where its employees will live surrounded by violence or hatred. It is sadly true that economic pressure rather than moral indignation often brings an end to such bitter human conflicts. It is particularly in those situations that we must remind ourselves that none of us are perfect. As childen, perhaps, we believed that all of human society could be neatly divided into "good guys" or "bad guys." As we grew older, we were disabused of this notion. We all have faults, and until we really accept this idea in our own minds, we can never peacefully negotiate as individuals, or groups, with those against whom we have grievances.

Prejudice threatens our national unity. Discrimination is synonymous with disunity, and it necessarily plays into the hands of our enemies. Over one hundred years ago Alexis de Tocqueville, a rather perceptive Frenchman, made the following observation: "If America undergoes great revolutions, they will be brought about by the presence of the black race on the American soil." It is a source of amazement to many people that the Communists have been so singularly unsuccessful in their attempts to recruit American Negroes.

Prejudice hinders our international relations. Members of

the white race do not reflect often enough that three-fourths of the people of the world belong to the so-called "colored races." The so-called "colored races" watch the United States carefully, to see if our practice matches our preaching. Whether it be pleasant to think about or not, Birmingham, Alabama, Cambridge, Maryland, Oxford, Mississippi, and many others, were fully reported and photographed by foreign newspapers. On these occasions, American law enforcement principles and techniques were subjected to world-wide inspection.

HOW PREJUDICE AFFECTS POLICE WORK

Prejudice of one group against another always complicates the police problem. Ordinary offenses are magnified. Incidents between individuals of antagonistic groups may lead to conflict of groups. Further, police are hampered by prejudiced criticism.

While prejudiced Whites will criticize the police officer for being fair, prejudiced Negroes will condemn him for fancied discrimination. This hampers the police officer in any case involving members of different racial groups because of the danger that an ordinary arrest, if regarded as discriminatory, may precipitate a racial incident.

Prejudice limits the officer's mental ability. Facts are the raw materials of rational thinking. We may be very intelligent, we may have learned carefully to limit our tendency to overgeneralize, and we may be reluctant to make conclusions on the basis of insufficient information. However, if we cling tenaciously to what we "know" to be true without, every once in a while, critically reexamining what we know, our attempts to think rationally will be fruitless. If we start with false premises, that is, facts which are not facts at all, we will come to false conclusions, no matter how sophisticated our process of thinking is.

As we consider some of the facts concerning the groups which make up our society, let us view them critically; that is to say, let us think of the methods by which these facts were established, the people who used the methods, and the kind of people who accept their findings as facts. It is obvious that each one of us cannot go through all the experiments and extensive observations which have been made in the field of intergroup relations. However, we can evaluate whatever has been done in terms of certain standards of objectivity and ability on which we can agree, and we can attempt to keep under control our tendencies to evaluate in terms of our preconceptions and emotions.

Nor is there anything shameful about accepting a new fact or suddenly realizing that we have been wrong about something. This kind of acceptance and realization is the very source of intellectual development. Intellectual development, like physical development, implies continuous change and adjustment to new conditions. It is usually the man who is unaware of his own attitudes, or is reluctant to admit to them, who will protest that he is not prejudiced. The man who knows himself a little better, and who understands the factors in our society which generate racial and religious prejudice, is not so eager to proclaim his freedom from prejudice. He is a little more cautious in his evaluation of his own behavior, and a little less afraid to admit that he has come under the same influences as his fellow human beings.

The person who has reached that point in understanding at which he is able to admit his own hostile and aggressive feelings, and understands a little bit about what causes them, can increase the proportion of reason in his behavior and decrease the proportion of emotion. He will not permit his feeling of hostility toward a member of a particular racial group to influence his behavior toward that person. He will recognize that sometime in the course of his life he has learned to distrust Jews, but he will not permit this feeling of distrust to make him forbid his children to play with Jewish children. He will realize that, though he has learned to feel antagonism toward Caucasians, he must not repulse the overtures of friendship which his Caucasian co-worker makes toward him.

As we become more understanding of ourselves, and more willing to change in the light of new knowledge, so we become more tolerant of the difficulties which other people face in their interrelationships. We learn that there is just no use in condemning and rejecting a man because he says that he does not want to live in the same neighborhood with Negroes. We learn to respect the man who suddenly realizes that he is prejudiced and admits it. And so we come full circle in our pattern of reason; we use it to temper our perception of people who are different from ourselves, and we consider the real significance of racial and religious differences. Again, we use reason to evaluate our own behavior and the behavior of those who have made us what we are, our relatives, our friends, our loved ones. Reason makes us doubt that our way is the best way, the right way, the only way, and doubt brings changes in our way of thinking and acting. Then, again, reason comes into play in our relationships with people and helps us to understand those who are prejudiced and to try to help them.

For government to serve its purpose fully, it must not only apply the law equally and without favoritism, but is must also provide equal protection and service to all. This position can be accepted as an essential principle of the American creed. Nonetheless, diligent effort must always be applied to make this principle a fact of life to all of our people. Therefore, the law itself must be the rule by which we live and work. There can be no fact of a citizen's makeup, color, religion, or economic or social stature, that will change his relative position under the law. Poor man, beggar, merchant, or thief, although they may conduct themselves differently or hold different beliefs, are each entitled to a common application of the law. It thus becomes imperative that while on duty the individual officer submerge any of his prejudices and beliefs which are contrary to the law and contrary to the above principle.

There is no race, creed, or color when the action of law enforcement becomes a duty and a responsibility. Police officials throughout the nation recognize this in a remarkable way. A law adopted legally by the people is for *all* those people. Each local police officer so employed takes a solemn oath to apply that law without prejudice or favor to *all* the people.

The police agency's protection and service must be allocated equally and applied freely to all. The agency serves all of the people and neither the status of an individual citizen nor an officer's attitude toward him should influence the agency's kind or level of service.

PREJUDICE IS NOT INEVITABLE

All this is not to say that prejudice should be accepted as inevitable. What we are trying to do is to understand all the factors which go into the formation and maintenance of prejudice. Sometimes, people who consider themselves broad-minded and tolerant tend to condemn prejudiced people because they do not throw off this early learning. The contention is that, when a man has lived to maturity and has learned more about life and about people, he should exercise his free will and rational powers and make up his own mind; he should not continue to govern his behavior by what he learned as a child. The choice, they say, is his, and so is the blame if he chooses the wrong point of view. However, before we condemn, we ought to try to understand the factors which cause prejudice. Only if we understand the factors can we figure out ways of combating them. For example, an understanding of the motives and feelings involved in prejudiced behavior has encouraged scientists to go one step further and develop a method for dealing with prejudiced persons in certain situations. Reactions to responses made to anti-Semitic remarks have been systematically observed, and it has been concluded that the most effective response is the unemotional, matter-of-fact statement of a bystander that, "We don't go for that kind of talk here." Such a rejoinder raises the morale of the Jewish person who has been insulted; it demonstrates to the other bystanders that everyone does not agree with the anti-Semite; and it may cause the anti-Semite to think twice before he insults someone publicly in this way again.

The person who says, "We have always had prejudice, and we always will have it; it is a part of human nature," is using the same kind of argument which prejudiced people use to justify their attitudes. The past is no map of the future. A clear picture of the past helps us to understand the forces and events which have led us to the present, and which we must consider in planning for the future. However, just because we have had a situation in the past, or we have it in the present, is no indication that we must throw out our hands in despair and refuse to try to change that situation. We have learned much about human behavior, and we are learning more every day, and we can use what we have learned to change behavior for the better.

Chapter 4

MINORITY GROUPS

INTRODUCTION

T HE TERM *minority* refers not so much to the manner of people in the group as it does to the status of the group members, how they are looked upon by other members of the culture, and how they are treated. Thus, a minority group is any distinct group toward which others have prejudices, i.e., preconceived ideas about what the group as a whole is like.

Minority groups are set apart from the general population by differences in race, color, religion, language, other cultural characteristics, or occupation. It is this "difference" that is used as a peg upon which to hang prejudice. It therefore logically follows that from a problem standpoint, the most important differences are those of race or color because these surface differences are highly visible, permanent and inescapable. Every member of a distinct racial or color group can be usually instantly identified.

What constitutes the minority, of course, depends on geography and who makes up the majority. In the United States, Negroes, Jews, Catholics, Puerto Ricans, Mexicans, Orientals and American Indians comprise large minority groups. In different areas and at different times in our history, eastern and southern European immigrants, people from Ireland, rural migrants, and newcomers have been accorded the treatment of minority groups. They have been looked down on, prevented from engaging in certain types of work, been kept out of some schools, churches and places of recreation. They have been told, directly and through certain actions, that they were not as good, as clean, as intelligent, and as capable as other people. Some have been rejected because they are supposed to be cheats, overambitious, or dominated by foreign powers. The same groups are accused of being seclusive and interfering, both overaggressive and naturally subservient, both hostile and happy-go-lucky. Such patent inconsistencies in their attacks do not bother prejudiced people. They are against groups outside their own, and they will believe the most contradictory statements about those groups, as long as those statements fit in with their negative feelings.

COMMUNITY ATTITUDES TOWARD MINORITIES

The extreme view expressed by a small vocal part of the so-called "dominant group" is one of complete and angry bias. They feel that the minority, in being different, is therefore lesser. Although biologists tell us that there is only one species—man—this antiminority group feels that their "position" entitles them to first choice in education, housing, employment, and preferential treatment in any situation.

The second attitude one encounters is a generally passive one. A common characteristic of this attitude is reflected in the statement, "I don't care what they do as long as they don't bother me." It is this group that usually claims a lack of bias and prejudice, and in many cases this is true. Many of these persons, of course, are unaware of what problems really confront minority groups. They were born into the dominant group and their contacts with other individuals and groups has been devoid, generally, of conflict and tensions. Theirs is more a position of not knowing, rather than not caring.

A third attitude consists of an attempt at an objective and progressive approach. These persons have learned that there is no "lesser man." Experience has shown them that all persons—Mexican, Indian, Protestant, Catholic, Jew, Negro, White—are equally capable of enhancing our culture. Science has proven that adequacy of learning depends upon adequacy of teaching. Therefore, when opportunities are open to all, equally, the end result can only be one of mutual benefit. This group is making an honest effort to identify and understand the problems of the Negro in order to establish a favorable community atmosphere where opportunities are open to all who are willing to work for them.

THE EXISTENCE OF DIFFERENCES

Racial, religious and nationality differences do exist. Why should we minimize this fact and try to obscure it by maintaining that all people are alike? All people are not alike. As a matter of fact, every individual is different, in a great many respects, from every other individual.

Police identification records clearly testify to this. Given a set of characteristics, an IBM machine can, in seconds, pick out from hundreds of thousands of individuals only one who has all those characteristics. Identification and apprehension of criminals would be an impossible task without the existence of many differences between individuals.

It is reasonable, then, not to deny that differences do exist, but to determine how important a particular difference is in our everyday interrelationships. First, however, let us discuss some of the areas of difference.

Race

The term race has many meanings to many people. To some it simply means a group of people descended from a common ancestry and consisting of persons who have similar physical characteristics. It is in this sense that many speak of Caucasians, Indians, or Negroes. Others tend to think of races in terms of nationalities, such as Italians, Greeks, or Norwegians, insofar as these names denote people coming from various countries or cultures. When majority and minority groups live side by side, a person who essentially is similar to those of the majority, but who has a trace of the minority-group characteristics frequently is grouped with the latter. Even competent anthropologists are not in agreement about what constitutes a race and what distinguishes one race from another. Mingling of human stock has gone on throughout recorded history, producing neither superior nor inferior types. Rather, the relative distinctions based on so-called racial characteristics (such as color of skin, hair, etc.) continue to become more obscure until now it can be said that there are no pure races; all races are intermingled.

It is significant that no basic psychological differences between so-called races have been scientifically established. Superficial differences do exist, tend to become exaggerated, and produce commonly accepted stereotypes. It can, in fact, be reasonably concluded that greater psychological differences exist among people of each race than exist among races.

Superiority of one race over another, long an emotional crutch for the personally inadequate and a rallying cry to international conflict, simply cannot be demonstrated. Like it or not, depending on our personal convictions, it can honestly be said that we are "brothers under the skin." To be very specific, the "knowledge" we commonly hold about race is really an impression of attitudes that we have come to accept and a product of what we have learned to believe.

Ethnic Group

An ethnic group is a human group bound together by ties of cultural homogeneity. Complete uniformity is not essential, but an ethnic group is likely to be marked by a high degree of loyalty and adherence to certain basic institutions, such as family patterns, religion and language. The ethnic group may even regard itself as a race, a people with common ancestry, but the fact or fancy of such common descent is of much less significance than the assumption that there is a blood relationship, and the myths which the group develops to substantiate such an assumption. The term, accordingly would include such groups as French Canadians, English Canadians, Welsh, Flemish, Walloons and the like.

Nationalities

We have a tendency to think of the people of each country as having certain national characteristics. We often lose sight of the fact that, even when there are such things as national ideologies and national standards of behavior, by no means all of the people in any country may be said to exhibit the same behavior. In addition, behavior which is characteristic of a particular nation will change when individuals change their country of residence. For example, many people who have never eaten hot dogs or sandwiches will begin to do so when they come to this country to live. So, too, patterns of speech and body movements which accompany speech are modified and adapted to the place where the individual lives. Certainly, the children and grandchildren of those who have changed their country of residence show few or none of the patterns of behavior of their forebears.

That people from different parts of the world are somewhat different in attitude, behavior and dress is obvious. We must, however, bear in mind that such differences are in no way an indication that one nationality group is either better or worse than any other nationality group. Speaking Italian in this country may be different, but it is no more different than is speaking English in Italy. To mainlanders, Puerto Ricans may appear talkative, but who is accused more often than touring Americans of loud and endless talking?

The point is, people often consider each other in terms of stereotypes. There is the loud, garrulous, patronizing American, the penny-pinching Frenchman, the reserved Englishman, and so forth. Yet there is no evidence to substantiate such stereotypes; there is, certainly, no evidence which indicates that all the people in any one country conform to a particular behavior pattern. There is even no evidence to support the belief that most of the people in a country conform to a particular pattern. Just a superficial acquaintance with a number of citizens of any other country will quickly reveal that there is a wide range of individual differences, just as there is in the United States.

A person is not only Irish, or Mexican, or French, or Puerto Rican. These nationality descriptions cover only a very small part of the whole person. People, in addition to being members of certain nations, are also parents, teachers, bookkeepers; they are kind, unkind, happy, unhappy, uncertain, and self-confident. They like to dance, or to play golf, or to read, or to watch television, or to go to soccer matches. A person is, in most ways, very much like all people, altogether different from every other person.

There was a time when we in this country believed that the best thing that immigrants could do would be to become like everyone else in this country as quickly as possible. We realize now that the people who come here are already like everyone else. We know that the differences in language, some food habits, and some other behavior are interesting and attractive, and that there is no very great reason for unlearning them unless individuals particularly want to do so. What we speak of now is no longer the "melting pot," into which all kinds of people go and out of which they come exactly alike. We are more interested now in cultural pluralism or cultural democracy, in which differences are accepted as valuable, and similarities to the working out of problems of common interest.

Color

The difference which people probably notice most often is the one involving skin color. To this difference are attached all kinds of ideas in the minds of people in this country, ideas ranging from relative intelligence to relative body odor. Now, though differences in skin color undoubtedly do exist, there is no valid reason for concluding that, because a person has a somewhat darker skin, he is less intelligent than people with somewhat lighter skin. There just is no connection between skin color and intelligence. Nor is there any connection between skin color and cirminality, or skin color and ambition, or skin color and body odor. Intelligence depends on a combination of innate capacity to learn, opportunities for learning, and psychoolgical and physical readiness. Criminality and ambition seem to depend upon what people learn from those around them, how they are treated by society, and how they feel about themselves and their own chances for advancement. Body odor depends on how often one bathes, the existence of certain diseases to which all groups are subject, individual, not group, differences in body chemistry, and, with some cultural groups, the eating of certain foods. So it is with most other traits and abilities which we tend to connect with skin color.

The shapes of the nose, eyes and mouth are also differences which we observe and connect with personality characteristics. The habit we have of thinking we can read character through physical characteristics is related to an old superstition which seems to be retained in some form by many cultures. In Western culture, it has developed into a pseudoscience called physiognomy, which assumes that psychological traits are reflected in the shape of the different parts of the face. There is no scientific evidence for such an assumption.

The attempt to relate the shapes of the lips and nose to earlier, and inferior, forms of human development is a waste of time. It has been clearly established that no earlier form of human development exists today, that all people living today represent the same level of human development. Also, if we are to compare the physical characteristics of people with animals, it becomes apparent that all racial groups resemble apes, for example, in some way. The everted lips of some Negroes and the smooth, long dark hair of some Caucasians are examples of such similarities.

Hair texture is also a mark of difference between groups, and it becomes a sign of inferiority or superiority with many people. For one thing, because Negro people are so often looked down on in our society, they themselves have developed a desire and a need to be as much like white people as possible. Since most white people have straight or moderately curly hair, this has become the standard of beauty and desirability among many Negroes. Hair is either "good" or "not good," depending upon how closely it resembles the hair of Caucasians.

The present state of scientific knowledge may be summarized briefly and should be thoroughly appreciated by every police officer. If one has a preference for truth and respects the method of science, he should examine his own questionable ideas about the races in the light of these facts.

Biologically, physiologically and anatomically, there is a basic unity between people of all races and nationalities. People's bodies function identically, they are born in the same way and die from the same diseases, irrespective of race or nationality. Their physical structure is alike, all people being possessed of the same number of arms and legs and other physical members and organs. The physical differences that exist between races—color, texture of hair, facial features—are extraneous and superficial and could never serve as a basis for a belief in any funda-

mental differences between races of men. The fact is that
are greater variations in size, strength, agility, etc., within races
and nationalities, than between them.

Religions

In our discussion of races, we have tried to point out the
fundamental similarity of the various racial groups. The differences we do find are primarily superficial physical ones which
are not really important, except insofar as our prejudices and
discriminatory practices have made them important. When
talking about religion, however, we soon realize that the differences among the various religions are real ones, and any
attempt to conceive of them as "really all one" or as "believing
in one God" ignores the great variety of answers which may
be obtained from asking questions which concern the nature
of God, the meaning of afterlife, and the value system in this
life. Any approach to understanding through a unified concept
of the different religious groups is just not realistic. Each religion has its own set of beliefs, its own rituals, its own philosophy
of living. If they are similar in some respects, they are quite
different in most important respects. There is little to be gained
by saying that all religious groups should live in harmony because they are essentially the same. They are not essentially
the same.

The challenge in living in a society made up of many religious
groups lies in learning to live together and work together in
constructive harmony, despite the real differences in religious
outlook. Why do we persistently harbor the belief that it is
necessary for people to be as alike as possible before they can
cooperate in the many functions of everyday living? Unhampered
and enthusiastic disagreement is the life process of a democracy.
It contributes not only to individual growth and creativity, but
also to the creative development of the whole social order. We
must forever continue to disagree, argue, change our minds,
and begin again to disagree, or we will atrophy and die as a
civilization. Through it all, we must continue to associate cooperatively and amicably in those areas of living in which we
agree. If we live and plan and work together, our disagreements

will have a form and direction. They will result in constructive change rather than in destruction; they can bind groups more firmly to each other than can all the sweet exhortations to love everyone because we are all alike.

It is, however, one thing to learn to recognize and accept real differences between religious groups, and quite another thing to believe in the existence of certain difference which do not, in fact, exist. Often, people use these false differences as the rationalization for their antigroup prejudice. Here we can set the record straight by showing that these differences do not exist.

For example, some people have the idea that all Catholics believe the same way about all issues, that they are told how to believe about all things, and that, in any kind of controversy, Catholics will always unite and take sides against non-Catholics. This belief is undoubtedly greatly strengthened in the minds of people who know very few or no Catholics at all. As it is true that in church-related matters the members of any particular religious group usually do agree, just so is it true that in church-related matters Catholics, also, agree with each other. If this were not so, we would not have religious groups for very long.

However, as with all other religious groups, Catholics show a wide range of differences of opinion on all kinds of issues involving community cooperation, legislation, politics and so forth. They are members of all political parties; some are for separation of church and state, some are for more state aid to religion; some believe in working together with all community groups, others prefer to work only in Catholic community groups.

The essential problem in creating understanding and acceptance among the different religious groups seems to be how we can prevent the tendency to overgeneralize the differences beween these groups, even while we recognize the differences which do exist. A difference in religious belief does not automatically mean a difference in political belief; preference for a method of worship does not presuppose preference for either more or less participation in the activities which concern the community at large.

THE RELEVANCE OF DIFFERENCES

Now let us consider the significance of some of these differences in our everyday relationships with people. Just how important are the differences we have discussed, and what changes do they make in our lives, our behavior, our thoughts? Are we, perhaps, letting our feelings about these differences influence us to such an extent that we no longer think very clearly about them?

If we look at the matter reasonably, free from emotional influences, we can see that race, religion and national origin are just not important when we are choosing efficient and amiable co-workers, good neighbors, or valued friends. Much more important are high professional standards and ability, similarity of social goals, and compatibility of interests. After all, the policeman wants at his side a colleague who will not jeopardize his own life or that of his "buddy" by poor judgment, slow reactions and ignorance. These qualities do not depend upon the race, religion, or national origin of a person. The homeowner wants a neighbor who will maintain his property at the level which the neighborhood demands. The Negro family which moves into the house next door is not less inclined to protect its investment by permitting the property to deteriorate. Does it matter if the friend who enjoys the same baseball game or the same evening of bowling is a Catholic, a Protestant, or a Jew, a Negro, or a Caucasian?

Of course, differences in religion and national origin become significant in everyday relationships whenever the matter at hand is one of a religious or nationality nature. A Catholic and a Jew part company when their respective times come to attend religious services. The Jewish child and the Protestant child do not attend the same religious school. The person whose family came from Italy enjoys the company of other Italians so that he can refresh his memory of the language or reminisce about common national experiences. So it is with all differences of opinion and diversity of interests. In a situation in which the difference is operative, those who differ go their separate ways, but if they agree on other matters, their cooperation and congeniality continue in those other matters. If one man believes in the existence of flying saucers and the other does not, is this any reason for supposing that they cannot bear to live next door to each other? If one man is a Democrat and the other a Republican, does this mean that they cannot work efficiently as a team playing bridge?

Thus the great danger in group identification of individuals is that we are letting racial, religious and nationality identifications influence our attitudes and judgments in unscientific and harmful ways. If we do, we are making a great error, for we are using these identifications when they are not relevant. It is because of the danger of falling into this irrational stereotype that group identification is dangerous.

TYPES OF MINORITY GROUPS

Minority groups can be divided into certain basic types on the basis of their drive for or against assimilation. They are the following:

1. *Pluralistic.* The members of this group do not choose to divest themselves of their identity. Instead, they desire autonomy. They seek toleration and recognition by the majority.

2. *Assimilationists.* The members of this group have an end diametrically opposed to that of the pluralistic group, in that they wish to lose their identity by becoming a part of the larger society.

3. *Secessionists.* This group seeks political and cultural independence. Thus they strive to form new governments, such as the Zionists and Israel.

4. *Militant (Dominant).* This group chooses to retain its identity forcefully. Their objective is to dominate or control others. The Nazis and Black Muslims are typical examples.

EFFECT OF PREJUDICE ON MINORITY MEMBERS

What happens to the personalities of those who are forever being blamed for what is wrong with the world? We can only say that it is surprising that most minority-group individuals are able to live reasonably satisfying lives. Plagued by labels of inferiority, criminality, dishonesty and overaggressiveness, most members of minority groups continue to work hard, rear their children to be useful members of society, and, in general, to live according to the rules. But it is not easy.

Belonging to a particular national or racial or religious group often means having attitudes and behavior which are somewhat different from those of other groups. The child of immigrant parents in the United States may be torn between loyalty to his family and the pressures outside the home to conform to the ways of this country. This conflict of desires may lead to the child's ultimate estrangement from the family even while he is not accepted by the new society. The resulting feeling of rootlessness, of not belonging, may cause delinquent behavior ranging all the way from truancy to acts of violence.

Minority Members' Reaction

Children of minority religious and racial groups early learn what it means to be a minority-gorup member, and may react accordingly. Their methods of adaption are identified with the following attitudes:

1. *Denial of Membership.* Perhaps the simplest repsonse a victim can make is to deny his membership in a disparaged group. This device comes easy for those who have no distinctive color, appearance, or accent, and who do not in fact feel any loyalty or attachments to their group. However, often, the member who denies his allegiance suffers considerable conflict. He may feel like a traitor to his kind.

Denial of one's membership may be permanent, as when one is baptized into a different faith, or succeeds in passing as a member of the dominant group. It may be opportunistic and temporary, as it was in the case of Peter, who under emotional stress denied that he was one of Christ's followers. The denial may be partial, as in the case of an immigrant who finds it expedient to anglicize his foreign-sounding name. A Negro may try to remove the kinkiness from his hair, not because he really expects to "pass"—but because a token escape from his handicapping characteristics is somehow symbolically satisfying.

2. *Withdrawal and Passivity.* From time immemorial slaves, prisoners and outcasts have hidden their true feelings behind

a facade of passive acquiescence. So well may they hide their resentment that to the superficial eye they appear completely satisfied with their lot. The mask of contentment is their means of survival.

Passive acquiescence is sometimes the only way in which seriously threatened minority groups can survive. Rebellion and aggression would certainly be met by fierce punishment, and the individual himself might succumb to mental illness induced by constant anxiety and anger. By agreeing with his adversary he escapes being conspicuous, has no cause for fear, and quietly leads his life in two compartments: one among his own kind, one in the outer world. In spite of their conflicts, most Negroes are mentally healthy—perhaps because acquiescence is a salutary mode of ego defense. One who develops a withdrawn and supine manner may be actually rewarded with a certain degree of protection.

Another type of withdrawal is found in fantasy. In real life the despised person may not find the gratification of status, but he may imagine, and possibly talk with his equals about, a better state of life than he enjoys. Like a cripple, he pictures himself as free from physical defects. In his dreams he is strong, handsome, wealthy. He has grand clothes, social position, influence, and the cars he drives are powerful. Daydreams are a common response to deprivation.

Withdrawal may also take the less pleasing form of cringing and sycophancy. In the presence of members of the dominant group some victims of prejudice try, as it were, to eradicate their own egos. If the master jokes, the slave laughs; if the master storms, the slave quails; if the master wants flattery, the slave gives it.

3. *Avoidance.* Many minority-group members avoid the unpleasantness of dealing with the dominant group by minimizing contacts which may hurt or humiliate them; many become shy and withdrawn. They develop their own communities and businesses where they need not deal with members of the so-called "majority." Others avoid identification with their own minority group by "passing" into the dominant group (light skinned Negroes who pose as white). Upper-class Negroes, especially

those in the business or professional groups, often tend to insulate themselves from contacts with whites and certain other Negro groups. Finally, there are those who retreat into a make-believe world and shut out the realities of their day-to-day existence.

There seems to be some idea that there is an inborn desire to stay with "one's own." Now, although it is true that some people react to prejudice and discrimination by trying to avoid the dominate group and to stay where there is less danger of such treatment, not all minority-group members react in this way. The necessity for clustering together is usually forced on minority-group members when they are excluded from the activities and facilities of the majority group. Thus, many anti-integrationists look at the pattern of separate facilities for Negroes and whites and insist that Negroes prefer it this way, that they would rather be with "their own kind." Similarly, Jews and different nationality groups are thought to be clannish and unwilling to be assimilated into the general cultural pattern. This is an example of circular thinking. These people are excluded from full participation in the general culture and then are accused of reluctance to participate.

If one were to examine the history of the Jews in this country, one would see a consistent pattern of exclusion practiced against them. From the "gentlemen's agreements" which prevent them from buying homes among non-Jews, from the clubs which turn down their membership applications, from the hotels and resorts which refuse their patronage, Jews have learned to keep to themselves. In spite of this discouraging history, there are still a great many Jewish people who do not travel in exclusively Jewish circles. Many of them risk rebuff and insult, but persist in their attempts to travel and associate freely. Assuredly, this often results in a somewhat less comfortable existence than is a life among "one's own kind."

Others may reject white culture as alien and champion black nationalism as a solution. They may even reject members within their own or other minority groups who fail to subscribe to the same doctrine.

Finally, they may rebel in the form of direct aggression. It may be overt and vocal, in the case of a "race man" (a professional champion for equal rights), or it may be overt and physical. Although the symptoms and effects of agitators may frequently become a matter of police concern, it is the fringe groups who experiment with dangerous violence who create the most serious challenge to a peaceful society.

4. *Self Hate.* Sometimes people may think that there is some basis in fact for prejudice. Even members of minority groups often begin to have doubts about their own groups. They must say to themselves, "I know I'm not dirty—or shrewd, or sly, or overaggressive, but so many people think my group is this way, maybe there's some truth in it. Maybe most of us are pretty hateful." What may develop in minority-group members, then, is something called self-hate. Fearing that there is some truth in the allegations of prejudiced people, hating that which, in themselves, can identify them as a minority-group member, and guilty because they are rejecting their own group, these people find it difficult to live at peace with themselves.

5. *Militancy.* Minority-group members may refuse to "take it." They may fight back whenever they can. Psychologically this is the simplest response of all. One who conceives of himself as hated by another and believes that he has given him no cause for hatred, will hate that other in return. In psychoanalytic parlance, frustration breeds aggression.

6. *Enhanced Striving.* To redouble one's efforts is a healthy response to an obstacle. People admire the cripple who has persevered and overcome his handicap. Such direct compensation for an inferiority is the type of response our culture most highly approves. Accordingly, some members of minority groups view their handicap as an obstacle to be surmounted by an extra spurt of effort. In every minority group there are many individuals who adopt this direct and successful mode of compensation.

7. *Symbolic Status Striving.* Contrasted with this direct and successful striving, we find a variety of off-center efforts that victims of prejudice may make to gain status. Sometimes minority-group members are especially fond of pomp and circumstance. One sometimes notes similar pride and polish in the processions, rituals, even in the funerals, of immigrant

groups. And the flashy display of jewels and expensive autos on the part of the *nouveau arrivé* may be a way of saying, "You held me in contempt, now look at me. Am I so contemptible?"

8. *Neuroticism.* With so much inner conflict to contend with, one wonders about the statistics of mental health among victims of discrimination. On the whole, mental health in minority groups is not greatly different from the run-of-the-mill in society at large.

If any generalization can be made it might be to the effect that victims of prejudice learn to lead their lives under a condition of mild dissociation. So long as they can move freely and act naturally within their own in-group they manage to put up with rebuffs received outside. And they grow habituated to this slight split in their mode of living.

POLICE AND MINORITIES

Police officers will notice certain distinctive behavior traits of members of minority groups. It is of the utmost importance that the reasons for such behavior be correctly understood.

Behavior is not racial. Any differences in group behavior are due to differences in the environment. Prejudice and discrimination are important parts of the environment of minority groups and affect their behavior in significant ways. Members of minority groups are more than usually sensitive and defensive. This results from prejudice and discrimination against them. When people are made to feel, from childhood, that they are "different" from other people, they are bound to be affected in some way. Because minority individuals feel that others are prejudiced against them, they become apprehensive and continually fearful of insult or discrimination. Therefore, they often develop strong self-protective reactions.

When a person is treated as an inferior, he will begin to feel inferior. He may develop aggressiveness or shyness to cover up his inferiority feelings. This is not peculiar to minority groups. It is a universal human reaction. Anyone who feels insecure or inferior is bound to develop some defense mechanisms. Psychologists know that arrogance is more often than not a cover-up for an inferiority complex.

One aspect of the sensitiveness and defensiveness of minority groups which is of special concern to the police is the fear and distrust of police which these groups generally have. At times this deep suspicion and a deadly fear of all police officers is based on their whole experience. Far too often the police make no pretense of impartiality where minority-group members are concerned. Many police officers consider it their job not only to enforce the law but also to enforce "White Supremacy," and to keep minority members in their place. The result is that a minority member frequently regards the police officer as his mortal enemy. When he migrates to other areas where this is not the case, he naturally brings these attitudes with him. That is why the police have to watch very carefully not to identify police activity with a given minority group, giving them the impression that they are being singled out for special attention. Anything that looks like special treatment to them is discrimination, whether the action is good or bad.

This attitude of fear and distrust for the police, regardless of whether it is justified or not, presents a serious problem in public relations for the police. It must be overcome.

Chapter 5

MINORITY RELATIONS PROGRAM

INTRODUCTION

W E ARE REACHING in our clumsy way toward perfecting a society of equal men with equal opportunity. The way is not easy, but the problem is soluble, not insoluble, and the only effective way of solving it is through nonviolent tactics. The civil authorities must be ever alert against the irrational and emotional incitements of race baiters and religious bigots. The very security of the democratic way of life resides in effective safeguards against the loosening of racial, religious and nationalistic hatreds.

One might ask why the policemen should be concerned, for the primary responsibilities of the police do not include the solving of sociological problems. History has shown, however, that when problems arise in the community that other established agencies (schools, church, welfare, government, etc.) cannot cope with, the public always turns to the police for solution, or at least control. More than that, the police force represents one of the most easily identifiable authorities in any society. To many elements of our society, it represents the only authority against which they may rebel. This is certainly true in a highly segregated and concentrated minority-group community. Police authority inevitably becomes the symbol of what they consider to be the entire community's apathy toward them.

IMPARTIALITY

The average citizen's respect for the authority of society is dependent upon the degree to which that authority is impartially exercised. This is especially true of the members of the minority groups, who may have little reason to respect law if it is apparent that they do not receive equal protection from the authorities who are administering it. The impartial enforcement of the law builds necessary respect for the authority of society. Only by commanding such respect can a police officer begin to cope successfully with the various conflicts which may arise between social groups.

A principle which each police officer must keep in mind in his dealings with people is that before the law men can be treated only as individuals, not as members of groups. It is the individual man who violates laws, not the group to which he may belong.

The role of the police officer in these explosive situations is admittedly a difficult one. On one hand, as a person, he is a product of the same social experiences to which all of us are exposed. It is possible, therefore, that he has absorbed some of the prejudices toward minority groups. However, as an officer of the law, and as a member of the police profession, he must stand as the symbol of the impartial authority of society. There rests with him the task of peacefully mediating the antagonisms and conflicts between various segments of the community.

The police officer must bring under control his personal sentiments and prejudices and subordinate them in a truly professional spirit. In this manner, and only in this manner, will he be able to treat fairly and impartially with the contenders in any dispute.

POLICE PROGRAM

A good program of police and minority-group relations has always been essential to the good order of the community. It is even more essential today. Such a program should go far beyond merely developing closer relations between the police and minority groups. The police must take positive action to increase public understanding of the problems and difficulties of minority groups, and likewise of the valuable contribution individual members of those groups make to community life. Such publicity, based on facts known to the police department, would be valuable in producing community harmony and in helping to prevent serious clashes between members of different groups.

Although the police cannot control or solve the basic causes of antagonism between groups, their central role in the protection and securing of civil liberties makes them a rallying point in the mobilization of all forces in the community. They must therefore make every effort to cooperate with every agency that can attack the basic problems. They should welcome and participate in the development of a general municipal program in which all groups in the city will work together to solve the broad problems relating to housing, recreation, transportation and so on.

At the outset, some sad but hard facts must be recognized. Minority groups and members of minority groups have their prejudices just the same as everyone else. More often than not, the subject of their prejudice is the police officer. The officer must understand that there will always be individuals and groups in the minorities who will not treat him fairly because the cry of prejudice has come to have political, economic, or even psychological value to them.

There are also those who will attempt to evade their obligation to obey the law and to frustrate their criminal prosecution by raising the hue and cry of discrimination, of police brutality, of prejudice. They must be made aware of the fact that minorities, too, must obey the law. They must realize that every right that our country gives us has a corresponding responsibility. The right of the individual ends where his responsibility to someone else begins.

MINORITY-RELATIONS UNIT

Because of the specialized and complicated nature of police problems, it would be feasible, and in some cities highly desirable, to set up a minority-relations detail or department along lines similar to a juvenile-aid division or a crime-prevention squad. In a small force this special detail might consist of only one man, whereas larger forces might find it necessary to develop sizable units.

Functions of the Minority-Relations Detail

The minority-relations detail is first a public information activity, acquainting minority groups with police policies, procedures and tactics. Where necessary, it interprets specific police actions, explaining why they were necessary and how they were taken. Second, it establishes and maintains communications between police and the minority segments of the community, the minority press and key individuals in the human relations field.

Third, the detail transmits information in the other direction, keeping the police staff informed about minority group and intergroup problems and activities, problems and activities that might otherwise remain undetected. The police are sometimes overly suspicious of a group's militant efforts, seeing in them a threat to order which does not actually exist. The two-way communication furnished by the detail brings the facts to both sides.

Fourth, the detail reports any police activities which are discriminatory, or may appear to the community to be discriminatory. It reports police practices which incur unfavorable public opinion.

Fifth, it operates as an intelligence listening post well situated within the framework of the community to receive early warning of trends and activities likely to result in civil disorders. In a recent instance, these officers were informed that racial violence was brewing at a school. A quick investigation indicated the situation was critical. The detail flashed the word to citizen groups organized to combat just such emergencies. Affected police field units were placed on a standby basis. The result— this detail, working with citizen groups, contained the situation. Finally, it can provide members for, and work in close coordination with, the community-relations unit which could be organized as part of the community civil action program.

Personnel

The unit should consist of well-trained and experienced police officers who have displayed an ability to meet the public and have a favorable reputation. It is profitable to assign to these specialized units officers belonging to minority groups. They are more sensitive to the problem, have previously established contacts in their community, and encounter fewer barriers. However, it must be emphasized that the officer's competency, and not his ancestry, is the overriding consideration in making the assignment. Community-relations details are not "window-dressing," they are not publicity gags designed to display minority officers in key positions. They are units charged with a grave responsibility, the successful performance of which may mean the difference between a stable community and chaos. In addition to police officers, it may be advisable to include such professional personnel as sociologists and psychologists, who may be employed for this purpose or may be citizens of the community who will volunteer their services in an advisory capacity.

INTELLIGENCE

Information is the key to the effectiveness of this unit. If a police force is to cope effectively with the many aspects of relations between different groups, it must know where trouble is most likely to occur and be able to act with great speed and flexibility. This ability is especially necessary when tensions are high or actual disorder has occurred. The information required for such speed and flexibility suggest the advisability of calling for special reports on intergroup relations for the use of police officials who are directly concerned with these problems. In a small city it might be a sufficient precaution if the chief periodically ordered special reports from patrolmen on the state of the opinions and attitudes of the people on their beats toward other groups in the community. In larger cities or places where many different groups live, however, the police need more specialized and constant information about possible trouble areas in order to do an effective preventive job.

Every race riot is preceded by a flood of rumors, expressions of increasing antagonism between groups and an increase in the number and intensity of clashes between members of antagonistic groups. By developing adequate methods for obtaining and recording the necessary kinds of information, the police can tell approximately how much danger of a riot there is at any given time, what group would start it, who their victims would be, and where violence would be most likely to break out. Such knowledge would be invaluable both in preventive work and in handling any disorders that might occur.

Danger Areas

It is essential, in the first place, to know where the danger points and areas of the city are. To get this information, all police incidents involving trouble between members of different groups should be recorded, perhaps on a spot map of the city. Such incidents would include cases of vandalism, traffic accidents that led to arguments or name-calling on a racial basis, other arguments witnessed by policemen or in which they had to intervene, fights between members of different groups and so on. The record should give the precise location of each such incident, the groups involved, the disposition of the affair, and any additional information that might be useful in preventing further trouble.

Group Attitudes

The second basic requirement for adequate police information in this field is current knowledge of which groups or neighborhoods are developing dangerous attitudes toward one another, and which ones are becoming friendlier. Such information could be obtained by requiring patrolmen in certain areas of the city to make regular reports regarding intergroup relations and attitudes on their beats. A special form developed for these reports would provide for the recording of such information as follows:

1. Current stories about recent incidents (which might be real or rumored) showing either antagonism or liking for some other group of citizens, approval or disapproval of actions of the city government, inculding the police, etc.
2. Rumors of activities planned by neighborhood groups against each other or outside groups or vice versa.
3. Complaints about any condition in the neighborhood or in the city which the people on the beat feel is disadvan-

tageous to them or advantageously to some group they
dislike.

4. Evaluation of the effects of any efforts being made in the
neighborhood by individuals or organizations to change
the attitudes of local people toward any other group in
the city, either for the better or for the worse.

Minority Incident Report

Every patrolman should be required to record all incidents
involving minority group relations in his area. Warning incidents
occur most frequently in buses and streetcars, subways, and
"els," in crowds, in stores and theatres and on the street. Thus
the cooperation of the transportation authorities and other
members of the community should be obtained and reports
obtained from them. Such strategically located persons as school
teachers, community workers, ministers, transportation employees, housing directors and social workers, along with officials
of the police department, should offer comprehensive and important information on tensions and possible developments.

The sources of all such information should be protected.
The information should not be used against individuals nor
given any publicity. It should be available only to authorized
members of the police force who need such information to
carry out the program of improving relations between different
groups. Such reports should include the following: (1) What
took place? (2) What appears to have set off the incident?
(3) Where did it take place? (4) Who were the parties to the
dispute and what others were involved? (5) Other details.

Emergency Reports

In addition to these general reports which would be periodically required of patrolmen in selected areas, all police personnel
should have standing instructions to report immediately any
sudden developments that might result in a serious clash. Such
reports should be promptly routed both to top police officials
and to the relations unit.

Handling the Reports

These reports should be sent directly to the minority relations section which is charged with their processing. In interpreting them, a middle course must be steered between the complacent dismissal of a given report as of no consequence and the hysterical overrating of every report of friction. Such a balance can be accomplished through developing a perspective on events by comparing them from month to month and from year to year over a period of time.

Evaluation Report

All of this current information should be regularly summarized and made available to designated police officials. One series of reports might deal with the state of public attitudes and rumors summarized by neighborhoods in such a way as to show changes and trends. A cumulative spot map could be used for recording police incidents, observed clashes or arguments. Widespread current rumors and other current information might also appear on the map. The original records should be indexed before filing so they can be quickly located if necessary. The unit should also maintain a map of the city or county indicating the location of settlements of different racial groups. The minority unit must keep their superiors advised of the results of this reporting.

Biracial Indexes

Through the use of statistics on arrests, reported difficulties on buses and streetcars, in stores and restaurants, in schools and factories, records of industrial absentees and school truancies, and similar developments, an index can be established that will give a rough composite "reading" on the comparative calmness or feverishness of the biracial situation at frequent intervals. If staff and funds are available, this device would be made more useful by preparing biracial indexes for each area of the city so that the fever spots may be localized and may be related more easily and directly to local problems of immigration, housing, employment and antagonistic elements.

Public Opinion Polls

While public opinion polls yield merely a report on "surface reactions" to questions put by a stranger, they do measure the extent to which race tensions under such conditions are being verbalized in public. With some qualifications, opinion polls can furnish a useful "running check" on developments, in terms of such significant social groupings as area, employment, age, sex, religion and race. Naturally, great care needs to be exercised in the construction and pretesting of questions and in the selection and training of interviewers as well as in the mechanics of sampling. Fortunately, in many cities fairly adequate organizations exist through which interviewing services may be obtained at less cost than would be involved in setting up one's own system. Such an arrangement has, however, the disadvantage of making one dependent upon the relatively untrained interviewers found in many such organizations.

Race Sentiments Barometer

Competent reporters will be able to send in shrewd qualitative estimates of popular sentiments and tensions that should give more adequate assessments of biracial tendencies than either the index or the polls. Such a race sentiments barometer, quantitatively rough though it must be, can estimate the intensity of emotional drives, and this will furnish a dimension not revealed by either the index or the polls. The index, in other words, can be used to sum up the current behavior situations; the race sentiments barometer can give a basis for a more fundamental diagnosis and a more accurate prediction through determining the power of the emotional drives at work, the significance of the societal and psychological "ground swells."

Specific Intelligence

In addition to these overall assessments of mass behavior and emotion, information should be compiled continuously on the specific program activities of antiwhite and antiminority leaders and organizations. When they give statements, picket minority or white meetings, organize publicity efforts, start to expand their organizations, or whatever, immediate estimates of the effect and success of such actions should be made available to those who are entrusted with implementation efforts. In addition to the immediate use of such reports, they should be suitably filed in order to give a more and more detailed picture of the prejudicial activities of intolerant and subversive white and minority leaders and groups. It is quite possible that some such dossiers will eventually accumulate and present a composite perspective that none of the individual items could reveal: a picture of antisocial activity sufficiently damning to warrant legal indictment and trial.

LIAISON

The first step in any program to reduce and eliminate minority problems is to contact and establish a working relationship with responsible leaders among minority groups. Benefits of liaison with such groups are as fololws:

1. Establishes a communications line for the airing of complaints and the enlistment of support.
2. Presents an opportunity to find out basic community problems and efforts which might be undertaken to correct them.
3. Furnishes the information necessary to establish policy for the handling of anticipated problems.
4. Furnishes the law enforcement agency with a cross section of community opinions and interests.

Establishing rapport with all organizations can build a reservoir of information about the forces operating in the community and provide the police administrators and community leadership with adequate appraisals of the tensions existing in the community and intelligent suggestions for an interagency or intergroup approach to relieve existing tensions. It can provide the police administrators with valuable insights about the community view of the effectiveness of the police service. This support can also provide an opportunity to interpret to these organizations existing practices of the police department, the reason for any policy changes, and the responsibility of these organizations in the total effort for the overall protection of life and property.

The importance of the juvenile division in this connection

should not be overlooked. No matter how the problems of juvenile delinquency and its prevention are handled by a given police department, the officers who are carrying out that program should be required to tie it in closely with the program aimed at improving relations between various national, racial and religious groups. A great many of the conflicts which lead to serious clashes between such groups are started and carried on by children and adolescents. In a race riot, moreover, the majority of the active participants are under twenty-five and many of them are around fifteen or sixteen years old. It will be readily seen, therefore, that if the juvenile division does a good job of handling situations involving group antagonisms, a great deal can be accomplished toward the reduction or elimination of dangerous situations and attitudes. Moreover, if such antagonisms are gradually eliminated among adolescents, they will eventually be greatly reduced in the entire community as these youngsters grow up.

The minority-relations unit must also maintain liaison between the police and other agencies interested in developing constructive solutions to the problems of intergroup relationships. Members of the section should attend all meetings likely to result in racial tension. For example, organizations which advocate white supremacy, and organizations of minority groups which meet to discuss policy and procedures should be adequately covered by the intelligence section. In many cases it is not possible for a member of the department to attend such meetings, but constant effort will usually develop informants who are able to attend and who can then report to the police the actions taken by the groups in question.

Religious Leaders

In no field of world problems is the need for the application of strong religious principles and moral behavior more apparent than in the racial conflict area. It is therefore essential that any liaison and community-relations program should include the religious leaders of the community such as a ministerial association and other religious groups. Messages delivered to the community through the pulpit pleading for support of law and order and for an uplift in community thinking which would enable community to meet its problems better are invaluable.

Liaison with Minority Groups

Minority groups should be made familiar with the position of the police. Their full and constant cooperation should be sought in the maintenance of public order by exposing false rumors, identifying dangerous individuals, and notifying their groups of the position of the police. The police should attend meetings of minority groups and offer advice and assistance whenever possible. Where problems are identified that involve other departments of the municipal government—or other governmental agencies—the police should take positive action to bring the problems to their attention. Once accomplished, do not just forget it; follow through to insure that some positive action is being taken. Eventually the minority group will come to realize that the police are looking out for the minority's interests, and a feeling of trust and confidence will develop.

Establishing liaison with minority groups is not a simple matter. Usually the task is more difficult, and more errors are made in establishing contacts with the minority-group members than would be suspected. Frequently, calls for volunteer cooperation with the police go almost unanswered by members of these groups. The police want contact with the people who are the champions of the groups they represent, not the police's champions to the group. The police do not need self-seekers or persons of questionable background. While the police may be grateful for the "police buff," they cannot afford the luxury of accepting his generously prejudiced view of their problems. Often a serious mistake is made by designating an inexperienced, or publicity- or status-seeking member of the minority as the civilian leader, and expecting him to establish an effective organization. Often it is learned only too late that a group has no responsible leadership, only those who parade as such for their own gain.

The Overzealous

In every community there are overzealous persons who at

times allow their zeal to overcome their intellect. They often fail to realize that their activities are likely to lead to bloodshed. They can usually be made aware of this nearsightedness and persuaded by a frank and friendly approach on the part of law enforcement officials, who point out to them the possibly dangerous, injurious attitudes they are creating. Thus these groups must be identified and contact established.

Hostile Groups

Police liaison should be established and maintained with groups who do not like the police, as well as with those who do. By so doing, two important purposes will be accomplished. First, and of primary importance, the police can, by maintaining contact, initiate actions to turn hostility into friendship. Second, as a source of intelligence, the police must stay in contact to know what they are doing, what they are planning, what they are thinking. A basic military tactic is never to lose contact with the enemy, for once you do, you will not know what he is doing and you become vulnerable to a surprise attack. This tactic is equally applicable to police in their dealings with hostile groups. Prevent a surprise attack!

Persons Who Advocate Violence

A list should be compiled of all persons known to advocate the use of violence. Such a list should include names, descriptions, photos and records. These individuals should be watched as closely as known dangerous criminal suspects, particularly in times of threatened disturbances.

Hate Groups — Bigots

Groups emotionally anti-Negro and antiwhite flourish and die in many American communities. There are individuals and groups who have a deliberate interest in fanning the flames of nationalistic and racial hatreds. Often, they are interested in setting up scapegoats among the various nationality and racial groups. By this means, they are able to divert attention from their own questionable purposes. The idea of racial superiority and inferiority has become a powerful and dangerous weapon. It is used by groups seeking to divide the population on economic questions. In addition to breeding and sanctioning an atmosphere of intolerance, these demagogic groups also serve as rumor and propaganda mills. Such organizations provide both leaders and rank-and-filers who jump into any riot situation the instant the break against law and order has occurred. They sometimes go so far as to plan and direct mob violence, but more often they seize upon mob violence and race riots as an opportunity to demonstrate their power.

In regard to the symptoms of an impending race riot, the main thing to look for in connection with such organizations is a progressive tendency to operate more openly and bodily; to propagandize against Negroes and whites or other pro and anti groups, and to presume the existence of a greater degree of social acceptance for their views.

These groups, their leaders, and their membership must be identified. Their activities and plans must be known to the police so that early countermeasures can be taken.

Symbols

Be aware of the symbols in the community that serve as psychological rallying points for the different groups. These symbols might be a place such as a church or school; they might be a special time such as the birthday of a revered leader or the anniversary of the death of one who is now considered a martyr. Such symbols can become the focal point of action on the part of opposing groups.

All too often the group itself will sacrifice a symbol, indeed even an individual, to further its cause. Thus the assassination of one of the group's own members in order to create a martyr and a rallying point is not unknown even in this country. By the same token, the destruction of a group's headquarters, meeting place, or the bombing of a member's home by the group itself has occurred. The group does it because it knows the resulting sympathy will strengthen its position as well as encourage recruits and financial contributions.

ADVISORY AND TRAINING FUNCTION

The minority-relations unit should work with those in charge of regular or specialized training programs, so that all members of the force will receive adequate training in the field of human behavior and human relations.

INVESTIGATE RACIAL DISTURBANCES

This unit should investigate all racial disturbances or rumored difficulty. They should contact all concerned in these incidents, ferret out causes, and attempt to correct and bring about cooperation from both sides. Meetings may be arranged and both sides given an opportunity to express their difficulties. Whenever possible, it has proven effective to include in such a team a police officer who is a member of the affected minority group. The cause of the tension should be corrected, thus reducing the probability that a similar situation will recur.

CITIZEN ACTION COMMITTEE

In carrying out this work, the officers can be greatly aided by the citizens in the community if their cooperation and assistance can be obtained. The first step is making the community aware of the problems, interesting them in the problems of others which do or will eventually actually affect them, and finally enlisting their personal assistance in overcoming the problem. These interested citizens should be formed into an action committee that can be called at the first sign of trouble, much like the former volunteer fire departments. This committee should consist of housewives, storekeepers, teachers, lawyers, ministers. In effect, it is a cross section of the community. These "neighbors" will be far more effective than "outside experts," for people are more likely to work with, trust and believe their friends and neighbors than total strangers.

The thing to look for in these people is fair-mindedness. The wonderful things is that such people are to be found on any street, in every city and hamlet, and more than that, these citizens are willing to give their time and energy. Besides knowing local problems, volunteers have fresh ideas. But most of all, because of their reputations in their community for fair play, they will be able to reach the people.

When racial trouble develops, this committee will first act as a fact-finding body by contacting their fellow citizens in order to ascertain the facts. Naturally the nature of the true problem as revealed by these facts will dictate the procedure to pursue in solving it.

One method is to hold a meeting of those affected. At it they are allowed to express their views and fears. The committee should be prepared to supply facts and suggest plans to alleviate the tension. It should put these plans into play.

An effective technique used in the case of racial disturbances at school has been to break the feuding group up into small discussion panels consisting of members of both groups. Let them "talk out" their hate. This personal contact will in and of itself help to melt the tension. Once you understand another man, you usually cannot fear him. If you are not afraid of him, you do not hate him. And if you do not hate him, you are willing to work out some kind of compromise with him.

ENCOURAGE BIRACIAL DISCUSSION

The first urgent necessity is to bring about and encourage biracial discussion among community leaders. In many cities grievances develop among minority groups and grow and fester, and the resulting tensions suddenly break forth in demonstrations. The general population is not even aware of the specific causes of the trouble because the interested groups are not talking with each other. It must be emphasized that police have an ideal opportunity and patriotic obligation to display their traditional ability to persuade disputing factions to sit down together around a conference table and discuss their grievances. To the extent that this can be done in good faith, it softens or removes the necessity in the minds of the minority people to dramatize their problems.

BIRACIAL COMMITTEES

Many cities have organized biracial committees which attempt to solve racial problems and prevent them from becoming police problems. Unfortunately the designation "biracial" is misleading, for no connotation of race is intended. Nor is the term to be understood to restrict membership to only two ethnic groups, for it is intended that all groups should be represented on these committees. These may well take the following forms:

1. An official biracial commission can be appointed by the governor or mayor. On such a commission are representatives of the police department, housing agencies, fire department, public health agencies, employment services, recreational agencies, and educational departments. Normally under this type of organization the biracial commission is an official body of the municipal government and has appointed as its head an executive whose responsibility it is to coordinate the efforts of all of the agencies involved.

This body should have sufficient power and budget to serve as a means for coordinating these facilities of governmental agencies: fact-finding social workers—police, court system, investigators attached to other departments; analytical—executives and experts serving the appropriate departments; and implementational—all facilities, legislative, judicial, and administrative, capable of carrying out constructive interracial measures.

2. A civic biracial committee can be sponsored by leading civic, labor, religious, business and educational bodies. This biracial committee is composed of representatives of civic groups, churches, unions, business groups, lodges, women's clubs and parent-teachers associations. Under this form of organization there is also usually appointed an executive to fill the role occupied by his counterpart on the official commission. This organization can have the advantages of flexibility and informality usually impossible in a government instrument, and it can effectively organize citizen pressure behind the constructive projects of the commission.

The total functioning of the city must be taken into consideration in determining what type of commission or committee will work best. Every city has established a leadership, either formally or informally. Any biracial commission, if it is to have any great chance of success, must arise from this leadership. In some areas the city administration is recognized as the leadership of the city. In cities with a strong governmental organization a biracial committee established as an official organization of the city government will perhaps work best. In other cities where the leadership is vested in business leaders, the civic committee is perhaps more desirable.

Several cities throughout the country have unofficial citizens' councils composed of outstanding business and civic leaders. These organizations are nonpolitical and wholly unofficial. However, if they are properly established and adequately controlled from within, they can act to a certain extent as the conscience of a community. Those cities with such an organization have a ready-made vehicle for the establishment of a civic biracial committee. This committee can be appointed by the leadership of the citizens' council and should consist of men whose views and opinions are sufficiently respected that they are likely to be followed.

Any biracial committee must, of course, have representatives of all races as members. Those organizations from which such committees have sprung have expressed the opinion that it is not desirable for the citizen's council to attempt to influence the appointment of minority members to the committee. It is believed to be more efficient and more acceptable to the minority community if the minority group themselves are permitted to appoint those who will represent them on the committee. Both as a practical operating procedure and as a sound psychological principle, there should be equal representation from races.

There is much to be said for the organization of both types of committee. This common dual form of organization has been urged because the governmental commission may have prestige and power in the government but be politically handicapped in carrying on propaganda activities. The civic committee, on the other hand, even though it lacks governmental power, can organize educational and pressure activities that will probably be essential to the success of any race-riot-prevention program.

Both the official biracial commission and the civic biracial committee should also be given adequate legal and budgetary support. They qualify for prestige and influence to the same extent as other bodies confronting "continuous emergencies"— police, fire, city planning and education commissions and boards.

In any city with a sizable and unassimilated minority population, the time to establish such twin organizations is as soon as possible. Do not wait until your city has sacrificed citizens to mob violence in its first or second race riot.

Both bodies should stand "on their own" and not be subsidiary to other comparable government commissions and civic organizations. If they are to serve their necessary purposes, they must remain as independent and free to act as possible. To assure friendly coordination, they should have certain influential members in common.

Executive Officer

Above all, each of the organizations must have an executive who understands that "committees do not work," that committee members talk a lot, tell others what to do, and only occasionally undertake small assignments. The executive must understand that the real labor of accomplishment is his. He has to realize that it is up to him and his staff to learn how to function in the name of and through the medium of the civic committee or governmental commission for which he works. Such an executive will naturally also be a man who has had practical organizational and publicity experience in some such field as newspaper work, politics, salesmanship, or advertising. This will give him the essential grasp of the public relations implications of his program. Without such a grasp, many civic and governmental projects fail. The program for these two organizations must include three main functions, as follows:

1. Constant fact-finding.
2. Constant integration and analysis of facts.
3. Constant translation of analysis into things to do.

Constant Fact-finding

Essential to any anti-race-riot program is an accurate and constant evaluation of the racial tension that exists in the community. Without accurate firsthand reports, wishful thinking and prejudiced planning all too readily begin to flourish. To obtain accuracy, as many varied sources as possible should be developed, for the more sources, the less chance of biased and incomplete reporting and the greater likelihood of dependable information.

The program should also have informants whose normal functions bring them constantly into intimate contact with people scattered through a variety of occupations. They should be so chosen that their contacts will assure geographic, economic and social cross sections of the city's population. Such a reportorial machinery should therefore assure frequent and frank reports from selected social workers, ministers, policemen and policewomen, labor leaders, school teachers, physicians, bartenders, barbers, recreation supervisors, judges and others who have immediate and candid contacts with leaders and rank-and-filers among all racial groups.

When the dual system is used, plans must be made to exchange information between the commissions for the sources of both commission will vary. Thus by sharing, a more accurate picture can be procured. These reports should deal with the following: (1) opinions and sentiments; (2) rumors—the verbal "milling process"; (3) racial frictions; (4) demogogic groups; (5) juvenile delinquency; (6) police behavior; (7) overcrowding, and (8) employment.

Constant Integration and Analysis of Facts

The reports must be processed so that meaningful conclusions may be drawn from them.

Constant Translation of Analyses Into Things to Do

This is the function that is the end for which the others are designed and carried out. It is also the most difficult for the committee, for it calls for positive definitive action and not buck-passing. It is therefore essential that the committee provide persistent and effective follow-through at the very outset. Reject all panaceas as impractical. Segregation, in particular, must be rejected at the outset since the only practical preventive course is one involving thousands of workable adjustments which will, in effect, implement the Golden Rule and permit the growth of healthy race relations.

Requests for Official Action

Because of its official position, the biracial commission can make requests and complaints, and prepare directives that will command consideration within the city government and in other governmental circles—consideration that the resolutions of the civic committee cannot command. Such requests will naturally be as multifarious as are the necessary and expedient adjustments in race relations. They will involve projects ranging from the construction of public housing to the proper enforcement of some relatively minor city ordinance.

PUBLICITY AND PUBLIC EDUCATION

Through such channels as daily and weekly newspapers, radio stations, schools, churches, women's and men's clubs and labor unions, publicity materials concerning race relations should be given virtually incessant dissemination. This mass distribution of facts cannot be achieved merely through throwing memos into the laps of editors, teachers, preachers and program makers. To be assured of an adequate and reasonably continual acceptance of the messages, the police must translate them into the forms most easily usable by the news media.

Daily and weekly newspapers want well-written, accurate news stories from dependable sources that they can insert into their columns with a minimum of editing. They also want the "stuff" out of which editorial writers, columnists and feature writers can easily create the kind of articles they want to write. Radio and television stations do not want speeches, except in rare cases; they want attractive programs or inserts for existing programs that will make people want to stay tuned to their wavelength. Schools want timely teaching aids that will fit into existing courses, that will help their teachers do a better job with the mental and physical equipment they possess. Schools and churches, unions and clubs, can also be induced to utilize speakers whom they can schedule, preferably in advance, and whom they can trust to present before their respective pupils, parishioners and members an "acceptable message."

Frequent opportunities present themselves for passing on biracial information and ideas for action to those who can go out and transmit them to great numbers of other people. Immediate examples are teacher-training colleges, teachers' institutes, program-making conferences for club leaders, special short courses and the like for ministers, real estate operators, insurance salesmen and others. Suitable program materials can be offered free or at a nominal price in order to obtain widespread distribution of the message. Such materials may well include posters, play scripts, games, pamphlets, slide films and, if possible, motion pictures.

To get the most effective interracial understanding in the areas in which it is most needed, education and publicity efforts must also reach "the lower depths" of a community. In other words, means must be found to combat intolerance in the places where potentially the most riotous elements congregate.

PRESSURE ACTIVITIES

To combat riots, the police must learn how to turn organizational pressures powerfully into focus so as to direct them towards the accomplishment of needed objectives. Such pressures are useful to overcome the apathy of governmental agencies; to demonstrate to the community that antiminority and antiwhite leaders and groups do not represent majority opinions and interests, and even constitute a danger to the American way of life; and to obtain financial support for constructive programs.

The organization of such group pressures involves more than the simple expedient of sending a letter to the presidents of a list of clubs and asking for "suitable action." The project—a slum clearance, a recreational, police, or possibly a legislative measure—literally needs to be "sold" to the organizations in question; this sales work can be done most effectively as a part of a constant educational campaign that must have been in operation for a reasonable period of time before an actual request for pressure support is made. When such assurance of support and interest has been prepared, it should be possible to get barrages of wires or letters to legislators or other governmental functionaries; to arrange impressive delegations to attend hearings or to wait upon officials; to bring about the passage of publicity creating resolutions when such actions are indicated as desirable ones by the circumstances; to get financial aid; or to do whatever else may be indicated.

DEVELOP INTERGROUP RELATIONS

Those who object to programs in intergroup relations are fond of the maxim: "Time will change the situation." They seem to believe that, left to itself, the intergroup situation must necessarily improve. There is a gross fallacy in this belief which should be carefully considered. The fact is that people who are separated from each other by barriers of law or custom, or both, cannot engage in those very processes which are vital in developing understanding and acceptance.

People separated from each other do not have the opportunity to associate in the everyday situations which make up living. They do not speak to each other as equals, become aware of each other's feelings and beliefs, share each other's hopes and aspirations. No matter how friendly the white employer feels toward the Negro servant, the servant knows they are not equals, and the two men do not really communicate to each other those thoughts which are reserved for friends, relations and other equals. Since most white people have little friendly contact with Negro people who are of the same social class with the same educational background, they do not realize that Negro people are pretty much the same as they are in all the ways that matter. The same may be said of Negro people and their attitudes toward white people. The two groups do not know each other, and have no opportunity for getting to know each other. What happens is the result of this situation.

We can see what has happened in our own country. Because of this separation, generations have grown up with no real knowledge of each other except stories they have heard (which become distorted in the telling) and information they have picked up which is rarely based on science and fact. These stories and misconceptions grow into larger-than-life myths, horror stories and stereotypes, which "everybody" seems to believe, and which the individual does not often think to question. You may protest that this is not so, that you yourself have had unfortunate experiences with members of other groups, experiences which corroborate all you have heard about those groups. If we are to be objective, however, we must admit that we cannot interpret even our own experiences accurately if we are misinformed, frightened, or unaware of certain facts. Seeing may be believing, but often we see what we want to see—what we thought we were going to see.

This business of people speaking to each other across group lines, and understanding or at least trying to understand each other is the basic activity in improving intergroup relations. Above all, it helps dispel the fears that feed on myths and rumors. It helps correct mistaken impressions, it reveals facts, and, over a period of time, it eases awkwardness and self-consciousness. It helps people get to know each other. Our fear of a particular group will color all our reactions to it, influence all our perceptions of it, and will inevitably widen the gap between us and that group.

However, mere contact with another group does not necessarily give us a better understanding of its members. Contact must reach below the surface in order to be effective in altering prejudice. Only the type of contact that leads people to do things together is likely to result in changed attitudes.

Knowledge must be built on mutual respect and a realistic understanding of the problems, emotional and otherwise, which face both groups. An open mind, good will, and a willingness to meet the other fellow halfway is a must, if a better understanding is to be reached.

Thus the program must be designed to bring people of various groups together in a way that enhances mutual respect. It is not easy to do so, for artificiality may easily mar the effort. Many committees on race or community relations do not really engage in common projects of mutual concern. They merely meet to talk about the problem.

Psychologically, the error lies in the lack of concretely defined objectives. The focus is unclear. No one can "improve community relations" in the abstract. Goodwill contact without concrete goals accomplishes nothing. Indeed, lacking a definite objective goal, such "goodwill" contacts may lead to frustration or even antagonism.

To be maximally effective, contact and acquaintance programs should lead to a sense of equality in social status, should occur in ordinary purposeful pursuits, should avoid artificiality and, if possible, should enjoy the sanction of the community in which they occur. The deeper and more genuine the association, the greater its effect. While it may help somewhat to place members of different ethnic groups side by side on a job, the gain is greater if these members regard themselves as part of a team.

A specific technique for accelerating acquaintance brings together people of diverse ethnic backgrounds in a "neighborhood festival." The leader may start the discussion by asking some member to tell about his memories of autumn, of holidays, or of food he enjoyed as a child. The report reminds other participants of equally nostalgic memories, and soon the group is animatedly comparing notes concerning regional and ethnic customs. The distance of the memories, their warmth and frequent humor, lead to a vivid sense of commonality. Group customs and their meaning are seen to be remarkably alike. One member may start a folk song or teach the others a folk dance, and soon a general gaiety prevails. While this technique by itself does not lead to lasting contacts, it is an ice-breaker, and accelerates the process of acquaintance in a community where formerly only barriers may have existed.

BIRACIAL EXPERIENCES

Possibly the most dramatic kind of implementation for a biracial program is one that builds on this homely truth: "Neighbors, black and white, do not riot against each other." This principle has been utilized in another area by the National Conference of Christians and Jews—its demonstrations of the dramatic educational value of its "trialogue teams." These teams consist of a Roman Catholic priest, a Jewish rabbi, and a Protestant clergyman or of similarly representative laymen. These men speak together before wide ranges of audiences, in schools, public auditoriums, before clubs, labor unions, churches, lodges, civic associations and over the radio, and thus help to give people of different religious faiths favorable experiences in the human qualities of those professing other faiths. Similarly dramatic biracial teams would furnish a way of giving white and nonwhite audiences better opportunities to come into contact with outstanding people of the other race on terms of simple and effective equality and respect.

Other types of biracial experiences can also be arranged. They should all have as their goal the synthesis of neighborly attitudes for large numbers of people. They may well include joint meetings of nonwhite and white organizations, young people's groups, lodges, women's clubs, service bodies, with a nonwhite or white group serving as host and the other group providing dramatic or musical entertainment.

Among the most practical biracial associations are those made necessary by the conditions of employment. Employers, labor leaders, and joint employer-employee committees have done spectacular work in certain industries and cities in creating conditions that brought about the employment of white and nonwhite members with a minimum of friction and with resulting interracial neighborliness.

Do not try to go too far or too fast—or too slowly. All effective adjustments of human relations must take into account the possibilities—what can be done—in one's own city. The police must work with and through other community leaders, for through them the police can reach and obtain the support and sympathy of powerful segments of the community. Programs that sound too radical, that bring forward too many new features at once and without adequate preparation, and that require greater speed than the community will sanction may do more to harm than to aid the riot-elimination program.

Do not ignore the less cultured and even the stupid and depraved elements. These are the people who may terrify the community in the next race riot. What they think, what they do with their time, what can be done to restrain or neutralize their antiminority and antiwhite feelings should be primary concerns of an anti-race-riot program.

Do not ignore existing biracial organizations, especially if they have healthy roots. The promoters of a riot-prevention program can save themselves a lot of groundwork and the antagonisms likely to arise from duplication by pumping new life into an existing civic or governmental organization rather than by setting up a competing new one. This does not mean, naturally, than an unworkable program with incompetent functionaries should be perpetuated. Investigate the existing foundations and build upon them, if possible.

MUTUAL BIRACIAL PROJECTS

Bringing members of hostile groups together socailly to communicate accurate and favorable information about one group to the other or bringing the leaders of groups together to enlist their influence, is less effective than enlisting their mutual aid in achieving goals which have a compelling appeal for both. When groups are brought together to work toward common ends, hostility gives way as the groups pull together to achieve overriding common goals.

This is not necessarily the case when the groups merely meet and exchange information, for favorable information about a disliked group may be ignored or reinterpreted to fit stereotyped notions about the group. Similarly, leaders cannot act without regard for the prevailing temper in their own groups; but when both work side by side, favorable information about a disliked group is seen in a new light, and leaders are in a position to take bolder steps toward cooperation.

EMERGENCY COMMITTEE

If a sudden forecast of racial trouble arises and there are no standing committees to meet the problem, a special committee in interracial tensions should be formed. It will have two jobs: (1) exploratory, and (2) emergency planning. An emergency program requires specific and direct reporting and action. There is not time to wait for the more gradual—but in the long run more effective—processes of education, legislation, or administration.

The exploratory job of your emergency committee requires information on the current state of affairs in the community. This pulse-feeling just needs to be placed upon a somewhat more systematic and adequate basis. Part of the committee should be made up, therefore, of people whose work brings them into daily contact with symptoms of interracial tensions and who have shown sufficiently sympathetic and yet level-headed insight into interracial problems to understand the meaning of what they see and hear.

The emergency planning job demands the inclusion of leaders who could be helpful in preventing or suppressing a race riot if one occurred. These would probably be the mayor, police chief, head of the local state militia unit, superintendents of the public and parochial schools, outstanding Jewish, Protestant and Roman Catholic clergymen, and responsible leaders of the commercial interests, veterans' and youth organizations, minority groups, trade unions, women's clubs and other civic bodies.

A small working executive subcommittee, divisible into exploratory and planning groups, would give the whole emergency setup simplicity and effectiveness. On this executive subcommittee or steering body should be the "no-nonsense" boys who are used to handling practical problems and to getting results. They should immediately prepare a plan to meet the potential problem and take all necessary steps to implement that plan.

The use of the petition by minority or protesting groups should be encouraged whenever possible. This means of obtaining redress may be used only under conditions of impartiality of the police and other public officials.

Provide ways in which people of all classes, ages, or racial background can participate in accepted and desirable social behavior. Try to get everyone some sense of social status, some feeling that he personally belongs to and is important as a member of an accepted social group. Attach and encourage the mechanism of democratic choice to the solution of problems. So far as is possible encourage group decisions as contrasted with orders from above.

CONTROLLING HATE GROUPS

The events of recent years have spawned countless hate groups which preach bigotry. Because of their great threat to our way of life, they must be exterminated.

It is argued by many that one of the most effective weapons in use against such a group is truth. They cannot stand exposure to the world for what they really are. A fact too often ignored by those who favor indiscriminate exposure of the professional bigot is that the very act of exposing his calumnies often gives them further circulation. When such material is circulated, it reaches people susceptible to bigotry who, far from being repelled, discover to whom they may turn for more servings of intolerance. Any attempt to prevent the bigot from speaking will result in sympathy or possible violence that will in turn generate the desired publicity, and more important, contributions and followers to his cause.

The most effective method of defeating the hatemanger is to quarantine him. However, to quarantine successfully the vendors of group hatred requires self-restraint, patience and discretion.

An essential part of the quarantine is the cutting off of publicity. This can best be done by giving the bigot no opportunity to become newsworthy, which he will be if prohibited from speaking or if arrested. One must never forget that the ultimate decision whether or not to publicize a professional agitator rests with the publisher, editor, station manager or whoever in each instance decides what the particular medium of communication should transmit. It is altogether proper to provide information concerning obnoxious persons to those who have channels to the public, but furnishing information and explaining the harmful results of advertising the troublemaker are the only permissible steps in dealing with the press, radio and television. Any approach which an editor or broadcaster could regard as an attempt at censorship will inevitably boomerang.

Another move in the battle is to dry up the bigot's sources of income. Those who surreptitiously give funds or other assistance to promoters of racial and religious intolerance pose a separate problem. Telling the public about concealed supporters brings them to the fore. It is often possible to influence anonymous benefactors by giving the facts of their involvement in the nefarious operations to the public. The police may do the following:

1. They should observe the activities of hatemongers and be prepared to furnish adequate information to friendly inquirers.

2. They should privately expose to opinion-molders the character and the message of the rabble-rouser. This includes city officials and heads of organizations who might be persuaded by his misrepresentations to cooperate with him.

3. After a rabble-rouser has rented a hall, there should be no public argument about it. If the proprietor of the hall has an indisputable right to cancel, he is justified in doing so. But if cancelling provides a legitimate grievance for the hatemonger, he should not be asked to withdraw.

4. If a bigot or his literature is being promoted in the community, the situation should be used constructively to induce more people to interest themselves in projects for improving intergroup relations.

Insofar as the public is concerned, if law enforcement authorities issue firm and decisive warnings that violence will not be permitted regardless of the merits of the contentions on either side, one of the biggest and most important steps toward undermining the effectiveness of the hatemonger will have been taken. Most of the people in the community, even most of those who might actively participate in a riot once it got started, will agree in advance that rioting and other civil disturbances are profitless and should not be permitted. In other words, most of the people in the community will support the police in a strong and resolute stand against open hostility.

A public attitude of this kind must be prepared well in advance and it must be constantly reinforced through periodic repetition. If people are indoctrinated along these lines, in times of crisis there will be support for the police from the true and influential leaders of the community and a hesitancy on the part of people generally to join in the fray. This support and hesitancy may be all the police need to give them time to swing into action and effectively quell any developing disorder before it gets out of hand.

Chapter 6

NEED FOR A POLICE-COMMUNITY RELATIONS PROGRAM

INTRODUCTION

T HE FIRST STEP toward an effective public relations program is the recognition of the need for such a program. Everyone in the field of law enforcement should be painfully aware that the need exists. The apathy and indifference which is more and more displayed by the public, the open hostility toward the police of a substantial segment of society, the more and more common and often-heard charge of police brutality, all are indicative of a weakness in the vital link between police and the public.

A primary responsibility of local and state police is to maintain law and order. The police can best perform this vital role when they have wholehearted support of all segments of the community—civil organizations, church leaders, public officials, business leaders, news media and other responsible members of the community. Indeed, a law enforcement agency cannot function effectively if the public is antagonistic to its basic aims and goals.

It is necessary to begin with the recognition of the fact that effective police work cannot depend simply on the use of night sticks or the threat of force. It demands the active collaboration of the citizens and of their community organization. Indeed, if we were to rely on direct police action alone, democracy would fail. Our republican form of government would collapse without voluntary conformity by the major portion of our society.

Every police officer knows how important it is to receive information from the citizens of the community. Indeed he recognizes that the solution of countless crimes and, more important, the successful prosecution of them is dependent upon the cooperation of the average citizen.

How well the ordinary citizen does his part in law enforcement depends on how well he knows his role—and how he feels about the police. Willing compliance with the law, of course, is the ideal way of enforcing the law. Actually, police agencies function most effectively and efficiently where there is mutual understanding of both community problems and police responsibilities. Such understanding provides the necessary basis for effective action to maintain law and order successfully.

The police and the public are not mutual antagonists, but should be mutually helpful to one another. The police are the public and the public is the police. Our law enforcement system is based upon the idea that a policeman is also a citizen, a citizen performing the law enforcement function for the benefit of himself and his community. The need for establishing better public relations grows with the increasing urbanization of our society. Among the many characteristics of metropolitan expansion is the widening gulf between public officials and citizens, who usually find themselves separated by the concomitant functions of specialization and diversification. Whereas face-to-face contacts are still the rule in small towns and villages, the inhabitants of the city tend to have less and less direct involvement with policy makers and administrators in the various departments of municipal government.

Over and above that, the department estranged from the people it serves is a most inviting subject for an "exposé" whenever newspaper circulation needs boosting. On the other hand, the morale of the police is always enhanced by virtue of community cooperation. The morale of the community is raised also.

REASON FOR POOR POLICE-PUBLIC RELATIONS

That the police are disliked throughout America, there can be no doubt. Many polls have proven conclusively the existence of that dislike. The public, with some justification, has come to think of the policeman in terms of some very unflattering stereotypes. Modern standards of selection and training have sought to rid the police profession of the gum-chewing, sarcastic, wise-cracking, slovenly, "chip-on-the-shoulder," ignorant, bullying policeman. Yet the stereotype persists in cartoons, jokes, moving pictures and other media of public information, which depict the police officer as somewhat less than the ideal professional, public servant.

It may be anomalous, but the better educated citizenry often regards the policeman as gruff and ill-bred, of low mentality, doubtful honesty and scant integrity. It considers him an uncouth, aggressive, rude figure of brutality, a frequently sadistic individual who chronically harasses the innocent citizen.

The educated citizen should know better, but law is an abstraction that usually becomes personified when its representative, the policeman, undertakes to enforce some law restricting behavior. Then even the law-abiding citizen starts to look upon the policeman as an enemy. Nobody likes to be stopped for speeding, much less for other more serious offenses.

Naturally we ask why does this problem exist? The answer is not simple, nor is it found in one cause. History paints the background of the modern problem. The police in our past seemed like a foreign invention imported from abroad, un-American, and generally held in low status in the society. The police force was frequently the scapegoat for all sorts of other difficulties and it did not seem to be the best agency by which the community could make its will for the respect of law felt.

Loss of Sustained Personal Contact Between Police and Public

The links between the police and the communal organizations have not been strengthened in the last quarter of a century, and in some ways they have been weakened. In an earlier period the policeman walking his beat at least had a certain familiarity with the institutions of his own immediate district. He knew something about the actual people and the actual organizations in the district of the beat which he walked. The links between the police force and the formal associations of the community do not adequately compensate for the disappearance of that older and perhaps more primitive kind of relationship—the foot patrolman.

Psychological Reasons

There are also psychological reasons for the problem. There is a mistrust of power, a popular distrust of the kind of power that is being lodged in the hands of these police lest they have a kind of control not susceptible to the popular will. Certainly those who have experienced restrictive action by the police, and even those who perceive themselves as potential police clients, resent this intrusion upon the pursuit of their private interests. This resentment may foster efforts to neutralize further police activity. Individual experience are reinforced by history. The history of local police forces both here and in Great Britain is liberally endowed with incompetence, brutality, corruption and the influence of private interests. The extensive documentation of policing in totalitarian countries frequently reinforces the worst fears of relatively uncontrolled police power. Our recent preoccupation with the emotion-laden issues of racial segregation, civil liberties, increased official crime rates and corruption of those in authority, especially the police, has re-sensitized us to questions of the quality of police forces and their social responsiveness. The accumulative effects of fear, mistrust and disdain overshadow relationships between the police and others and result in restricted interaction between the two factions, incomplete cooperation and distorted perceptions of police motives and operations on the part of the public.

Police officers and their operations tend to be set apart because they are visible reminders of the seamy and recalcitrant portions of human behavior. In societies where a generalized stigmatization of the individual and perhaps his associates is the prevalent reaction to social deviance and where there is a pervasive orientation that "getting caught" is the crucial determinant of this degradation, the consequences of police detention and apprehension loom large, indeed. Therefore, prudence demands that actual or potential clients construct the maximum insulation between themselves and the police who are the pivotal figures in the application of social sanctions. The reservoir of possible police clients has grown immensely with the proliferation of legal regulations. Positive reaction notwithstanding, thoughts of policing to this segment of the population may conjure up images of surveillance, inconvenience, embarrassment, frustration and indignation. Though the presence of police may serve as a positive socializing symbol for social control, it may also be a constant reminder that the police must be isolated in order to reduce the risk of social sanction.

Isolation of Police

The rapid growth of professional expertise in a complex industrialized society has had its effect upon policing. Modern crime detection techniques, police administrative procdeures, techniques of handling mass demonstrations and riots, and communication networks have contributed to the increased differentiation of the role of policing. Good policemen must be trained and retrained. To the extent that such specialization creates an occupational structure with its own standards of behavior and a body of specialized knowledge, this occupation may be thought of as a profession. Professionalization to the point of being granted license to determine the content of policing provides both the condition and the impetus whereby the profession may become isolated from other occupations and the general public. Whereas the professionalization of other occupations might be looked upon as very desirable by the general population, its emergence here serves to aggravate an already sensitive relationship between the police and the public. Becoming more expert and unreproachable in the restriction of behavior may be interpreted quite negatively, especially by those who were not in sympathy initially with police procedures and philosophies.

One of the most important contributions to police isolation stems from the general policy, official or unofficial, of policing organizations themselves. That is, in the interest of "good police work," officers are often advised to isolate themselves from certain segments of the public in order to avoid entangling or contaminating relationships. In fact, becoming closely identified with any segment of the public is frequently condemned because of the increased vulnerability to charges of favoritism and the fear of incurring obligations that subsequently could become detrimental to police operations.

Literature, Movies and Television

Most conceptions, and misconceptions, of law enforcement are derived from motion pictures, television shows and mystery stories. There have been many times, certainly, when law enforcement officials have gritted their teeth at the televised inadequacies of Mr. Hamilton Burger. Because of these fictional portrayals, the best thing any person can do is to forget what he has seen and heard and just start afresh. It should be pointed out that the Keystone Cop was just the figment of a film director's imagination; that the loud-mouthed, red-faced, fat bully in uniform, if he ever existed, is a thing of the past. Even on the constructive side, the new, clean-cut, clever sleuth of the television crime series is a streamlined and oversimplified portrayal of the modern detective. Yet the myths persist, and the overdramatized portrayals of the past, plus the few misfits of the present, have succeeded in cruelly smearing the ordinary policeman, in fact, the entire police service.

Deliberate Smear

Unfortunately, the true image of law enforcement is being unfairly distorted and smeared today as never before in our history. Those who enforce and administer the law find themselves the targets of ridicule and contempt. There are those who wish, first, to convince the public that the police are their enemy, not their protector and, second, to shackle, neutralize, frustrate and demoralize the police themselves. The serious consequences of this type of attack cannot be overestimated. It strikes at the very foundation of our democratic process and could, if successful, so weaken the structure of our government that the rights of all citizens to the pursuit of life and liberty would be jeopardized. Part of the distortion is being created by certain groups to weaken the democratic process. The small groups of critics, however, are more vocal and vociferous than the police supporters, so that the first impression is one of widespread condemnation of police. This is not true, but the campaign of vilification has left policemen puzzled, bitter and deeply resentful.

Corrupt Cop

Nor can we ignore the corrupt cop, for the misdeeds of one policeman stain all policemen. No other group in civil service or industry carries the shame of a member longer and strives so earnestly to win back the loss in public confidence that such an act causes. Sadly enough, those who are responsible for providing the material for the smears are the small number of men within the police ranks who have betrayed their trust out of greed, unconcern for their oath of office and the public welfare, and with cynical disregard for the fine records established by thousands and thousands of devoted police officers. This type of man must be weeded out and brought to justice, quickly and effectively. It must be made emphatic that law enforcement, as well as the public, will not tolerate this type of behavior.

Lack of Knowledge

Much of the lack of confidence and respect is based on a lack of knowledge. Greater efforts must be made to inform the public of our aims and accomplishments, particularly at this time.

Whatever the voices speaking out at this time, their comments about police have brought reams of newspaper space, hours of air time, and miles of photographs of and about the men in blue. Such attention has made many people realize that they know very little about the men they pay to protect them.

To most people the policeman is part of the scenery; they see him but seldom have any dealings with him. Occasionally, a citizen is shocked by the intrusion of a policeman into what he regards as his private life, an intrusion he deeply resents, when stopped for jaywalking or when given a summons for a traffic violation. For the most part, however, even at this point the policeman is regarded as a necessary but annoying part of the modern municipal picture.

LEARN WHAT THE POLICE IMAGE IS NOW

Whatever the cause, an image does exist. The first job of the police is to discover what it is. They must appraise the relationship which they presently have with the public. It can become a bombshell in itself, for it demands a recognition of the fact that there is no unanimity, rather there are numerous distinct and widely divergent groups. Next, these various groups must be identified. Only after that can a meaningful search be undertaken to ascertain the opinions and attitudes, as well as the depth of conviction of each group. However, such must be done, for any successful public relations campaign must be directed to specific groups in an attempt to create or alter equally specific opinions.

Many times, police agencies call in the "outside experts," or the "special survey group." Others use systems ranging from questionnaires mailed to each residence within their jurisdiction, to the "educated guess."

No single method is best; however, it is wise to bear in mind that human beings resent an improper approach to determine their thinking; tact should be the keynote.

COMMUNITY RELATIONS

Police-community relations means exactly what the term implies—the relationship between members of the police force and the community as a whole. This includes human, race, public and press relations. This relationship can be bad, indifferent or good, depending upon the action, attitude and demeanor of every member of the force both individually and collectively.

Public relations is a term often used interchangeably with community relations. In the popular and more correct sense it means the positive cultivation of opinions favorable or at least not antagonistic to the group seeking the particular relationships. Thus, if a public relations counselor would define "public relations," he would likely say, "It is a planned program, or a system, designed to gain and hold the good will of the public." Thus, police public relations is the combined, deliberate, effort of all the employees of the department to implant in the minds of the people the idea that policemen are friendly, understanding, capable, and willing to be of service to the community.

Public relations is a continuous job of keeping the public informed of what your department is doing, with emphasis on the services it renders to the public.

Public Relations and Propaganda

Any discussion of public relations must also include a reference to propaganda, since the two terms are closely related and often erroneously thought to be interchangeable. While both terms refer to methods of influencing human attitudes and consequent behavior, propaganda is more concerned with actual control of the induced thoughts and actions. It might be said that influencing attitudes is the primary goal of public relations, but for the propagandist the emphasis is upon control of behavior. Propaganda has also been described as the attempt to create mass attitudes which will precipitate identical behavior in large numbers of people, and one writer has stressed that propaganda achieves these results by the manipulation of words and their substitutes. Perhaps a major characterization which differentiates between public relations and propaganda is the strong negative connotation which has come to be associated with the latter word. It is safe to say that while the public relations function has been accepted as legitimate by most people in the metropolis, there is a widespread aversion to the overt use of propaganda as a tool of influence.

Public Relations and Publicity

Neither is public relations exactly similar to publicity, although both functions evidence a preoccupation with molding public opinion. Publicity, however, is concerned even less with consequent behavior than is public relations, and is employed primarily to place favorable information before the individual citizen. Thus, while public relations is a two-way street with information and opinions flowing between groups, publicity is a one-way street along which information travels in a single direction only. A certain passivity is usually associated with the recipient of publicity, while the public relations function in most cases assumes that response and interaction will result.

Public Relations and Reporting

Reporting, unlike publicity or public relations, does not have as its major objective the alteration of attitudes or opinions, but is a more neutral function with the purpose of providing information. Public information programs are more likely to be accepted by citizens because they are less associated with the bias that accompanies publicity efforts. The consideration of consequent opinions which results in selective reporting, however, is for all practical purposes a method akin to public relations and publicity, for attitudes can be shaped by withholding pertinent information.

BASIC GOALS AND PROCEDURE

The basic goals of law enforcement with respect to community relations are threefold: first, to enlist community support as an aid to law enforcement; second, to overcome an individual's dislike or fear of law enforcement, and third, to eliminate abuses of police authority which serve to give credence to unfavorable attitudes existing within the community. These goals are achieved by a program which uses the following procedure:

1. Appraises community attitude.
2. Identifies community interests.
3. Relates department policies with community attitudes and interests.
4. Initiates programs of action to earn community respect and confidence for the department.
5. Actively seeks full public cooperation and support in the prevention and detection of crime, the protection of life, property and the rights of all citizens.
6. Seeks to further improve relations between the police department and the community it serves.
7. Seeks to create a better understanding of the problems of both the citizens and the department.

Police public relations is best studied, analyzed and measured by the effect it has on others. You can judge the quality of it by the effect it has on your public, and your progress or lack of progress can be measured by your public's reaction toward you and policing generally.

BASIS OF THE COMMUNITY RELATIONS PROGRAM

A good community relations program has three basic facets:

1. Training of officers, including training through discipline.
2. Public information activity.
3. Efficient police work.

Unless they are in existence and interworking, a community relations program does not exist. Training provides a base, but public information and line officers must supply to training that information which keys it to current needs. Public information is a useless activity unless it is backed up with competent line officers who are enforcing the laws equitably. The most dedicated line commanders can accomplish little unless training provides well-schooled personnel and public information creates a cooperative public.

An image of an agency gained through a formal public relations program can, at best, be of only superficial value if it does not reflect the actual worth of the agency. This, in essence, is the distinction between reputations and character. Reputation based on sound character has lasting value; reputation otherwise based is transient and of dubious value.

The police are a business and must sell their product which is service to the citizens, community leaders and officials. There must be good salesmanship based on an acceptable product in order to gain this confidence.

When these principles are recognized, it becomes clear that the best method of selling a police department is to convince the people the police have an understanding of them, and are thoughtful and considerate of them. Basically, police public relations is getting along with people. It is proving to people the police are working continuously in their interest. Sometimes it is not selling at all, it is "unselling." There will come a time when they will run up against a person who made up his mind long ago that he dislikes policemen. So, they have to "unsell" him on this idea before they can "sell" him on the idea that policemen, after all, are pretty good fellows.

RESPONSIBILITY

The chief of police is directly responsible for the state of police-community relations. The chief must train whatever personnel he has and require them to do the job they are capable of doing. No department or community can afford an officer who fails or neglects to promote good police-community relations. The police must be strong in their belief that they can always do much more.

DEPARTMENT MORALE

Because the attitude of the law officer is often mirrored by citizen attitudes, departmental morale is also an important factor in promoting good public relations. In addition, the more satisfaction an individual receives from his membership in an organization, the higher will be the number of contributions made toward the organizational purpose. Informal means by which police morale is heightened are extremely important, but unfortunately they are less definitive than the formal. For example, a sense of companionship both on and off the job often contributes to better performance, while hardship and frustrations in the home of the individual often make for a depressed and apathetic policeman. Admittedly, these indirect determinants of public relations are beyond official departmental manipulation.

Some of the formal determinants of police morale include departmental commendations for heroic or otherwise exceptional performance of duty, and job advancement for qualified individuals. An effective performance rating system will be welcomed both by supervisors and subordinates in the police organization. The publication of a newsletter and the maintenance of a recreation program including bowling, basketball and softball leagues as well as golf tournaments and sports banquets throughout the year will prove effective.

Chapter 7

FAIR, IMPARTIAL, EFFICIENT ENFORCEMENT

UNIFORM LAW ENFORCEMENT

T HE BEST PREVENTIVE for riot, indeed for all illegal conduct, is an outstanding law enforcement organization that has earned and maintained a reputation for fair, impartial and efficient law enforcement. By the same token, the keystone of community relations is good efficient law enforcement. Propaganda and public relations ballyhoo will not supplant it, nor will they suffice. Indeed, there is no substitute.

Law enforcement knows what must be done and has done it. Year in and year out, the police officers of this country have laid down their lives for the preservation of our government under the law. They will continue to do so, for this is the only course of honorable, dedicated men.

The police must enforce the law impartially, objectively and equally, regardless of race, creed or color. It must adhere to the standard long ago adopted that there is only one class of citizenship, one standard of police techniques. The policy of all police organizations must be explicit in what is expected of each officer. No division can be tolerated. The officer must realize that regardless of his personal opinions it is the responsibility of a truly professional police officer to enforce the law as it is handed down. This is absolutely essential in the normal, routine work day, but it assumes even greater importance when minority groups are involved. The activities of the police are subject to constant and close scrutiny, and any activity on the part of any police officer which could be interpreted as showing racial intolerance or bigotry is likely to be seized upon and used as a reason for condemnation of the entire dpeartment.

Impartiality is not always easy, or is it always popular or expedient, but it is the only course of action a department can follow and properly fulfill its responsibility to all segments of society. An attitude of impartiality will cause some members of the majority group to feel that the police officers are unduly protective of the minority groups. Such an attitude may even at times cause members of the minority group to feel that they are not being properly treated. The officer has the responsibility of rising above those pressures to assure that in every incident involving members of both groups which come to his attention his actions are beyond reproach.

Uniform Standard of Enforcement in All Areas and With All Criminals

There must be the same standard of law enforcement in minority group districts as elsewhere in the city. A strong program of preventive work should be undertaken in minority group areas, the same as in any other area of the city. Every violation in a minority area should receive the same attention and be handled in the same manner as a like violation in any other area. This will often require extra heavy policing of these areas, but this burden must be borne. The community must be shown that such action is taken in order to protect those who live in that area, not because it is a minority area.

The erroneous attitude that certain types of offenses should be condoned because "we can't expect too much from a minority group" must be shunned. The police cannot condone an attitude that the crimes of minority groups are relatively insignificant so long as they affect only members of the same group. An offense by a member of a minority group against one of the minority group must receive the same thorough attention as any other crime.

It should not need repeating that crimes committed against members of a minority, regardless of who the culprit may be, are just as unlawful, just as reprehensible, as those against any other human being. There must be no distinction drawn in the police handling of such offenses.

Distribution of Personnel

The distribution of the patrol force according to needs and hazards is one of the most important questions to consider in developing a police program designed to improve intergroup relations. In almost every city there are danger spots and areas where clashes occur repeatedly and other regions where interracial incidents rarely or never take place. Forces must be stationed accordingly.

It is asserted by some that intense police activity in a given area is psychologically disturbing to its residents. It is claimed that such policing adds weight to discriminatory beliefs held by some who witness it and creates a sense of persecution among those who receive it. Is the police administrator, then, to discard crime-occurrence statistics and deploy his men on the basis of social inoffensiveness? This would be discrimination indeed! This would be to abdicate one's responsibility! It would be a desertion of the good law-abiding people who must be protected.

No matter how critical an area may be, the majority of its residents want to be law-abiding citizens. These law-abiding citizens are the backbone of the neighborhood and must be protected. If these law-abiding citizens have just cause to feel that they have not received adequate police protection during normal times, it is not likely that they will depend on or fully cooperate with the police officials in preventing or stopping outbreaks of violence when times are not normal.

Danger Areas

Danger of interracial clashes is greatest in areas where there is incidental or competitive contact between groups that are antagonistic toward each other. The particular danger spots can be discovered by checking police records of clashes between members of different groups over a period of time.

Areas in which a minority group is displacing an old majority population are areas of likely conflict.

A plant or school located in an antagonistic majority-group neighborhood, where numerous minority-group members work or attend classes, is another danger area. In particular, the gates of such establishments and routes to and from public transportation may require special attention. Danger points are public transportation lines that pass through danger areas or carry mixed groups of passengers and transfer points where mixed crowds gather during rush hours. Public recreation areas, shopping centers and other places that are jointly used by antagonistic groups are danger areas particularly when the habits of using such areas are changing because of the use of the area by minority groups.

Police Preventive Action

Concentrating police at the potential danger points is useful at all times in preventing the development of dangerous antagonisms and may be imperative during periods of high tension to prevent riotous outbreaks. When sorties are being made by residents of one neighborhood against those of another, the most effective method of prevention may be to assign extra patrolmen to the aggressors' neighborhood in order to break up such raiding parties before they can get started.

ELIMINATE BIAS AND PREJUDICE IN THE POLICE FORCE

Because of the public position they hold, the police must refrain from any action or comment which would indicate prejudice or bias. Any activity on the part of any peace officer which could be interpreted as showing racial intolerance or bigotry is likely to be seized upon and used to condemn his entire department.

Thus, a police department's community relations program begins with the department itself with an impartial program of hiring, training and promoting and with a firm human relations policy and strong disciplinary machinery to enforce it.

Hiring and Promoting

Uniform minimum standards should be applied to all applicants for recruitment and to all promotions. Race, creed, or color have no part in either hiring or promoting; thus, they should not be the basis for refusing to hire or promote. On the other hand, an individual should be given no preference because of his membership in such a group, nor should the standards of the organization be lowered merely to allow the hiring or the promotion of any person.

There must be minimum recruiting standards, and these minimums must be held even though the department operates below strength. It is far better to have to increase unit output than to corrupt your department's future with substandard men.

Rather, the police must realize that a responsible and loyal employee is the most valuable asset of any organization. The needs of each position should be carefully considered and the qualifications predetermined. The following should be considered in selecting a police officer: education, physical fitness, character, intelligence, attitude, appearance, courtesy, maturity, personality, poise, assurance, tact, experience, and prior training. Recruit selection must be made solely on a merit basis, preferably by an independent civil service department. Only those meeting highest standards should be selected for public service.

The police cannot accept an applicant whose intolerance is so high it is a disabling factor. Where it is not too deep-seated, it can be erased or at least diminished. With policemen, as with society in general, our immediate concern is not in what the man thinks but what he does. The police must recognize only one class of citizenship—first class citizenship. Any incident of police action which deviates from this policy must be met with swift and certain discipline.

Discipline—enforced compliance with police policy—is a key which is available to every police administrator. It will work.

TRAINING

The program cannot end with impartiality in selection. Law enforcement has gone beyond the crude era of brute force. Now the officer is a professional called upon to meet the demands of a professional. This demands training and retraining.

The basic course must prepare the officer to meet the challenge of our modern society. This demands that a substantial portion of the program be directed to the consideration of community relations.

The purpose of training in the field of community relations is to develop the proper attitudes and behavior patterns. In certain instances this will demand the changing of already well established, but faulty, patterns. A frontal attack by way of lecture or command will usually be futile, indeed it will evoke hostility and cause the individual to search for reasons to justify his already established attitude. The program must therefore be so designed and presented to do the following:

1. Broaden the officer's range of experience.
2. Demonstrate that the faulty pattern fails to aid and indeed hamper law enforcement.
3. Show the officer that his attitude change will not alienate him from friends and co-workers, but rather that it will improve those relationships, will improve his skills, his chances for advancement, and public attitudes towards the force.

Generally, the objectives of the program can be summarized as follows:

1. The development in police officers of an appreciation of the civil rights of the public.
2. The development in police officers of the ability to meet police situations involving minority groups without undue militance, aggressiveness, hostility, or prejudice.
3. The development in police officers of an adequate social perspective. This objective involves the development of such behavior and understanding as the following:
   a. Being courteous and respectful.
   b. Refraining from name-calling and the use of epithets.
   c. Avoiding insults and humiliating citizens.
   d. Serving, guiding and helping others.
   e. Understanding the problems that many minority-group members encounter.
   f. Understanding the unique "cultures" of minority groups for a better understanding of their motives, desires and

overt behaviors.

4. The development in police officers of an awareness of individual and group differences and the ability to differentiate among individuals as personalities apart from their race, religion, or national origin.
5. The development of an understanding by police officers of how their words and actions may be perceived by and affect the public.
6. The development in police officers of an acceptance of integrated situations.
7. To develop in police officers a knowledge of the fact that their behavior will infuse similar intergroup behavior and attitudes in other members of the police force.
8. The development in police officers of a recognition and awareness of the role of associated community human relations agencies.
9. The development in police officers of the skills requisite for anticipating and meeting the police-human relations aspects of (a) their work; (b) incidents rooted in factors of race, religion, and national origin; (c) juvenile offenses; (d) civil rights complaints, and (e) community tensions.

Principles of Learning

In preparing and conducting any training program the following principles should be recognized and respected:

In deciding who should learn what, the capacities of the learner are very important. Brighter people can learn things less bright ones cannot learn; in general, older children can learn more readily than younger ones. The decline of ability with age, in the adult years, depends upon what it is that is being learned.

A motivated learner acquires what he learns more readily than one who is not motivated. The relevant motives include both general and specific ones, for example, a desire to learn, a need for achievement (general), a desire for a certain reward, or to avoid a threatened punishment (specific). Motivation that is too intense (especially pain, fear, or anxiety) may be accompanied by districting emotional states, so that excessive motivation may be less effective than moderate motivation for learning some kinds of tasks, especially those involving difficult discriminations.

Learning under the control of reward is usually preferable to learning under the control of punishment. Correspondingly, learning motivated by success is preferable to learning motivated by failure. Even though the theoretical issue is still unresolved, the practical outcome must take into account the social by-products, which tend to be more favorable under reward than under punishment. Learning under intrinsic motivation is preferable to learning under extrinsic motivation.

Tolerance for failure is best taught through providing a backlog of success that compensates for experienced failure. Individuals need practice in setting realistic goals for themselves, goals neither so low as to elicit effort nor so high as to fore-ordain to failure. Realistic goal-setting leads to more satisfactory improvement than unrealistic goal-setting.

The personal history of the individual, for example, his reaction to authority, may hamper or enhance his ability to learn from a given teacher. Active participation by a learner is preferable to passive reception when learning, for example, from a lecture or a motion picture. Meaningful materials and meaningful tasks are learned more readily than nonsense materials and more readily than tasks not understood by the learner. There is no substitute for repetitive practice in the overlearning of skills (for instance, the performance of a concert pianist) or in the memorization of unrelated facts that have to be automatized. Information about the nature of a good performance, knowledge of his own mistakes, and knowledge of successful results aid learning. Transfer to new tasks will be better if, in learning, the learner can discover relationships for himself, and if he has experience during learning of applying the principles within a variety of tasks. Spaced or distributed recalls are advantageous in fixing material that is to be long retained.

Subject Matter

The cadet must learn that people differ by race, religion, politics, economic status, occupation and in a thousand other ways. He must learn they have a right to be different. He learns that everyone is a minority-group member—that each of us belongs to many groups, any one of which can be and often has been discriminated against.

He must learn that many members of minority groups consider all police to be their natural enemies. This results from a tendency to attribute to the police of this state the same attitudes and conduct as were encountered at another time from law enforcement officers in other areas. Therefore, police officers should be instructed about the importance of cultivating the goodwill of such people and proving by fair and courteous treatment that the law and the people are their friends. To this end, police officers should receive training to equip them with a knowledge of the special problems and attitudes of the groups with which they deal, so that good will and confidence may be established and maintained by the efforts of every member of the force.

Background Information

To understand the problems of minority groups, new recruits should be given background information about them and the neighborhoods in which they live. Such material, which can be obtained from the sociologists of a local college or university, is more meaningful to the police recruits if it concerns an area in their own city or in the nearest larger city into which a succession of immigrant peoples have moved in the past forty or fifty years. This material can be presented by the regular staff of the training school. There is considerable merit, however, in the plan of having at least some of it presented by competent members of the minority groups in the community.

The specific background material to be used depends in part on what minority groups live in the city. Items in a required reading list should contain accurate and unbiased information that is not too academic or profound.

The training of police in the background of minority groups, in their relationships to each other and to the majority group, and in the areas of the city in which minority groups live should be designed to do the following:

1. Acquaint recruits and members of the regular force with the facts about racial similarities and differences. Emphasis should be placed on the point that scientists have found that no group has biological or racial tendencies toward criminality or delinquency.

2. Explain the large part that social and economic conditions play in determining the behavior of different racial, national and religious groups. Different groups who have lived successively in slum areas of different cities have been found to develop certain tendencies toward criminal and delinquent behavior as a result of living in such neighborhoods. In Chicago, for example, there is one deteriorated neighborhood which has been occupied by successive waves of immigrants—Irish, Polish Jews, Italians, Mexicans and finally Negroes. This neighborhood, no matter which of the groups were living in it, always produced a great deal of organized crime and gang activities.

3. Demonstrate some of the important contributions that members of minority groups have made to American life and culture.

The courses should include studies of the various pressures, behavior patterns and environmental reactions of juveniles and minority group members.

Indoctrination in Civil Rights Laws

All police trainees must, of course, receive a thorough indoctrination in the civil rights laws which they must uphold and which limit police authority. The Bill of Rights articles and amendments of the Federal Constitution, similar provisions in state constitutions, and summaries of Federal and state legislation, as well as city ordinances which have bearing on the rights and privileges of citizens should be presented to all police recruits both in lectures and in written form to be studied at their leisure.

A working knowledge of these legal bases of police work

is fundamental to every officer's understanding of his job, particularly in his relations with members of minority groups. Some system of examinations should therefore be set up to test this knowledge. For example, the examination might take the form of imaginary police situations and problems involving various points of the civil rights laws. Each officer could then be required to explain how he would handle each situation and to give his reasons.

The officer must be taught that these variations cannot influence him in the discharge of his duties. His department handles the people involved in incidents only according to the degree of their involvement. There is no other measurement. Existing laws are enforced and nothing else. We do not enforce beliefs or prejudices—including his own. He must realize and accept the demand that during his hours of duty, he is a composite of the entire community.

The cadet must be taught to translate his technical background into solutions of field situations—problems which involve people. Thus in these courses, sociology should be stressed more than ethnology; applied human relations stressed more than theoretical psychology. The purpose of the training is to provide immediately usable knowledge. Some consideration must thus be given to the various techniques that can be used to train the officer.

Discussion Group Sessions

In the area of police-community relations, the methods of police training and retraining should also be reexamined by local law enforcement. One method is to use small discussion groups led by section leaders trained in the fields of psychology, sociology, or the specialized field of minority-group relations. If an agency does not have an instructor who is well versed in this field, aid may be sought from professional teachers available at local colleges, universities and corporate training sections.

One way to conduct such discussions is to employ the "case method." In the case method, a real-life episode is presented. What each person involved in the episode did and said is given along with appropriate background information. Then a group discussion of the episode or case is held under the guidance of the conference leader. Each person in the group tells how he feels about the various acts and decisions of the people involved in the episode. Because of the nature of the cases, real differences of opinion emerge in the discussion. The exploration of these differences and their causes constitute an important step in the alteration of attitudes.

The case materials must not be ivy tower or academic stuff which do not apply to realistic police officers. They should be based on an analysis of actual incidents. Every effort should be made to insure their practicality and reality, so that officers are able to identify easily with the materials.

The case method is based largely on the "learn-by-doing" concept. Ideas and experience become connected. Moreover, by allowing the total group to participate, advantage is taken of the pooled effect of the group's experience and skill. Thus, anyone who can benefit from experience will profit from the course, and we can expect positive results with police officers.

The case method with its free, informal atmosphere and divergent opinions constitutes an ideal medium for raising doubt in the police officer's mind about his current improper attitudes. This is essential for little or no progress can be made toward revising a police officer's attitudes unless he can be made uncertain about his incorrect attitudes and how they may not square with the needs of the police department. However, if it can be shown to the police officer that his actions, as dictated by his attitudes, notions and points of view fail to help him to act effectively, attitudinal change can be achieved.

A new attitude, if it is to be accepted, must be developed together with a person's social and work group. If possible, a police officer group must take part in creating the new attitude. The case method permits this collaborative interaction. Moreover, as a police officer's attitudes change in the group situation, the change is seen as accepted by the group (non-ostracism) and as one which came from the group. Thus, the change is more freely accepted.

Furthermore, it has been amply shown that a prime factor in learning is motivation. One motivating force in police officer training is the usefulness of the course material to the on-the-job requirements as the police officer sees them. Therefore, any course must be presented in a manner that makes its applicability clear. The case method is an ideal vehicle for achieving this purpose.

Role-playing

Role-playing is a method being used more and more in education to involve and thus interest and educate the student. In role-playing, a situation which regularly confronts the police officer is described, and roles of the various characters in the incident are assigned to students who are to assume the role and attitude of the character. The students play their roles the way they think the actual individual would. Thus the student is called upon to project himself into the position of others, to "feel" the emotions and thinking of people who may be different from him. The theory is that the resulting understanding of the motives and actions of others will tend to modify his own attitude and better enable him to deal with the actual problem when it arises.

After the scene has been completed, there should be a group discussion and analysis of the behavior of the participants. In this manner, insights into his attitudes and interpersonal relationships are developed by the police officer.

There are several outcomes from this type of training. First, the police officer's attitudes towards his job need and job requirements are modified along desirable avenues. Second, skill in dealing with police-human relations problems of a practical, everyday nature is developed. Third, needed knowledge is incidentally acquired in a police-human relations context. Fourth, human relations thinking habits that are realistic and objective are developed. Fifth, preconceptions are replaced with understanding.

Fields Trips and Work Experience

One of the methods of teaching is to expose the officer to actual conditions. This can be done by field trips to minority areas and to businesses owned and operated by minority-group members who live within the area. A rotation system might be adopted whereby each officer-student would be assigned to work as a team member in the community relations section, or where he would work in conjunction with an outside social action agency, such as juvenile or adult probation, parole officers or the local welfare department, for a limited period of time.

The purpose of this approach would be to acquaint the officer with the motivations behind the problems he faces in law enforcement and it would also serve as a vehicle to introduce the human side of the officer to a troubled segment of society. This type of training would give the officers a greater insight into the problem areas of his community and of the people with whom he works.

Watch for Indication of Prejudice

The entire training staff must constantly be alert in the classroom, on the exercise field, and in the locker room, to discover signs of disabling prejudice which might make the cadet a poor risk. Conditions of tensions should be artificially created so that the man's reaction can be studied. Obviously he should not know that the situation is contrived to test him.

Instructors should watch for signs of friction between cadets who belong to different national, racial, or religious groups. If such friction develops among recruits, the men involved should be brought together before a superior officer. A strong effort must be made to reduce the friction to personal terms and to handle it on that basis. If, however, either cadet persists in displaying an antagonistic attitude toward an entire racial, religious, or national group, he is put on probation; and if his attitude does not change, he should be dismissed.

Obviously there must be no discrimination practiced in the handling of the cadets. This requires that a number of apparently small points be watched to insure equal treatment of all trainees. The assignment of lockers and seats in the classroom, for example, should be arranged on some impersonal basis such as the invariable use of alphabetical name order.

Special In-service Training

Police officials in cities that have grown rapidly and where interracial relationships are already tense, should consider the advisability of supplementing the training program suggested above with a concentrated brief course that could be quickly organized and administered to all police personnel. The aim of this supplementary program would be to highlight methods of handling immediate issues and problems in such a way as to minimize tensions and increase police prestige among those groups of citizens who seem most unruly and most likely to become involved in any public disorder that might occur.

This course should be developed by practical policemen and should be derived directly from their personal experience in successfully handling day-to-day police problems. The selection of the men best qualified to prepare this material is of the utmost importance to the success of the program. They should be the ten or twelve men on the force who, regardless of rank, have been the most effective in working directly with the groups about whom it is feared serious trouble may center. The final choice should be based on the recommendations of honest and trustworthy members of the minority groups involved. The policemen who will be able to develop the kind of a course here suggested will be those who have the confidence, respect and liking of the people on their beats.

The men thus selected to prepare the special training program should be relieved of their regular duties for a week or two. During this period they should meet daily with a social scientist who has both practical experience in dealing with minority groups and a broad understanding of their problems. The function of the social scientist would be to bring up general problems for discussion by the group of officers, to draw out the individual policemen regarding their experiences, to help the group arrive at common agreements regarding the best methods to use in the various practical situations discussed, and to systematize the results of these conferences in an outline or syllabus that would become the basis for the special training program. In all the discussions of practical police problems, particular efforts should be made to determine the methods that were most satisfactory to the people on the beat.

The special training course developed in this way could be given to the force in two to five periods of an hour or two each. It could be organized as a series of lectures but probably would be more instructive as a series of demonstrations of police incidents in which the trainees participate. These demonstrations might show wrong and right ways to handle various situations, each followed by a brief talk pointing out the differences. Some of the men who put the material together might be detailed to help train the rest of the force. The number of trainees at any particular session should be small in order to encourage group discussion of the various points brought out. For this and other reasons, the special course might best be given in the various precinct stations of the city rather than at headquarters or at the police school. In this event the training could be given first in the precincts where it is most needed and extended later to other precincts, or several teams of instructors could give the course simultaneously in various precincts.

Retreats

The use of command officers' retreats is another area of training which has been largely overlooked by law enforcement. Both the religious world and the business world have used this system of annual, isolated retreats so that their command officers might concentrate their efforts upon self-criticism and evaluation, retraining, exploring new developments, and as a brain trust to attack the various problems facing their organization. This approach appears meritorious and should be explored by the larger law enforcement agencies. Smaller agencies might try a joint retreat with neighboring agencies of the same size, or if an area is a rural community, perhaps on a county basis.

Follow-through Program

Human relations training, like any other training, will be most effective if it is periodically reinforced. This reinforcement can come from a program of posters, leaflets, statements at musters and communications from the top command. Additionally, a system of reward for extraordinary action in the human relations aspects of police work and the incorporation of these rewards in the performance record of the officer will be helpful.

TACTICS MANUAL

There are many advantages in bringing together in a brief manual or in a section of the department manual the methods to be used by the police in preventing or handling incidents involving minority groups. Such a manual would outline in concrete terms the basic policy of the department in various situations and thus serve as a reminder of important points and as a basis for enforcing discipline. It would, of course, be invaluable in both recruit and in-service training, and should be distributed as part of the special training program discussed in the preceding section.

The preliminary draft of the manual could be prepared by the group of officers who develop the program of special training in interracial relations. The contents would vary to some extent from city to city, depending upon the particular situations and problems of different cities and the varying characteristics of their minority populations. There might be some variations due to differences in state and local legal backgrounds. These points should be considered by commanding officers in approving the final form of the manual.

The manual probably should not be too detailed because no two situations involving antagonism between members of different groups are likely to be identical. However, concrete material on a variety of recurring incidents would help the average patrolman to see the application of the tactics manual to his job. Subjects to be covered in the manual would include methods of approach, handling of violators, informing all parties of their rights, handling of disputes, a policeman's responsibility in civil cases and practical psychology.

The general purposes of the manual would be as follows: (1) to make sure that members of the police force follow lines of behavior which enable them to perform their full duty without unnecessarily irritating or antagonizing members of any racial, national, or religious minority group; (2) to insure that police incidents are handled in such a way that everyone concerned will realize that the police protect the members of minority groups; (3) to enable the police to intervene between citizens whenever such action seems indicated or desirable to prevent arguments, disputes, etc., from developing on the basis of the race, religion, or nationality of any or all the parties involved.

ASSIGNMENTS AND ADMINISTRATIVE CONTROL

Assignments to various positions, patrols and shifts should not be made on the basis of race, creed, or color. Members of a minority group can be effectively used in minority districts, but should not be restricted solely to such areas. The use of integrated patrols in all sections has proved to be of tremendous value. It demonstrates to the community the impartiality of the police. All personnel must be subject to the same standard of administrative control.

MINORITY-GROUP OFFICER

There are great dangers in developing or allowing a minority-group policeman who is "the law in his area," "can square anything," is "real tough on the members of his race and they never complain." The minority-group officer should not be allowed to be the law unto himself. He should be a respected and supported bridge to his community, not a back door for removing administrative problems by methods that are largely extralegal. A police administration that casts its minority-group officers as back doors rather than as bridges almost forces them into being Uncle Toms, or politicians, or free lance opportunists making the most out of a privileged position. A temporary gain can sometimes be won by "back-door" personnel usage. A complaint can be "cooled" or an annoying local condition removed, but each such instance is another irritant in the police-community relationship, all the worse because it is temporarily buried.

Publicity

It is wise policy to give Negro officers and those who belong to other minority groups at least their full share of publicity. Such publicity helps to build up the morale of the entire minority group, and it also increases the respect and trust of that group of citizens for the entire police force. It also inclines all other groups in the city, including the majority group, to look more favorably upon the entire minority group.

SCREENING AND EXCLUDING
OF BIASED POLICE OFFICERS

Each police officer must maintain a professional attitude toward minority groups. Regardless of his personal opinions, it is the responsibility of a truly professional police officer to enforce the law as it is handed down. The importance of all adhering to these standards cannot be overemphasized. For it is well known that the activities of the police are subject to constant and close scrutiny. Any conduct on the part of a single officer which could be interpreted as showing racial intolerance or bigotry is likely to be seized upon and used as a reason for condemnation of the entire department. It is the responsibility of police administrators and supervisors to take appropriate action to see that all officers adhere to this standard.

Chapter 8

COMPLAINTS AGAINST POLICE

INTRODUCTION

M ANY CITIZENS in the community will not talk about alleged improper or poor police service; many silently blame the police for conditions that are not police problems at all and rightfully belong in some other city agency; many cannot articulate their complaints, and many others tragically are resigned to a notion that they can expect nothing positive from the police department. The end result is detrimental to the police, for the airing of grievances—real, fancied, trumped-up or the result of vicious rumors—is necessary to reach any kind of understanding and to keep the community temperature down.

The law enforcement agency must satisfy the community that it has established adequate procedures to prevent unfairness and excessive use of force, and that it will impartially investigate all complaints and take remedial action where necessary and justified. Each citizen must be convinced that the local law enforcement officers are interested in protecting the persons, property and legal rights of all citizens in the community.

The police must therefore acknowledge criticism of police practices and examine the areas and practices criticized. If the officer is wrong, the supervisor should make it known to the proper authority and take appropriate action.

The quailty of police work must be constant. It must be emphasized again and again that public respect must not only be earned but maintained. Close supervision and strict discipline of police personnel is absolutely vital. Any and all allegations of irregularities, misconduct, or improper use of force by police personnel must be thoroughly investigated and appropriate action

121

be taken. Thus, the procedures available to investigate citizen complaints of police misconduct are of critical importance in community relations because, if persons who believe they have been treated unjustly have no forum which they trust to explore their claims, their attitude of distrust is never dispelled.

A properly administered complaint review system serves both the special professional interests of the police and the general interests of the community. As a disciplinary device, it can promote and maintain desired standards of conduct among police officers by punishing, and thereby deterring, aberrant behavior. Just as important, it can provide satisfaction to those civilians who are adversely affected by police misconduct. In serving these ends, complaint administrators must not impair the effectiveness of the police as a law enforcement organ. At the same time, due to the exceptional powers of the police and the impact on individuals inherent in their work, the civilian community's interest in police activity should not be underestimated. Public confidence, vital to an effective police department, can be fostered by a well-run and well-publicized complaint-review system.

Departmental personnel should understand that complaints of improper action by police officers are to be carefully investigated. It is unfortunate that in many departments either the complainant is entirely wrong and the officer blameless, or the complaint is justified and charges must be prepared. Often such all-or-nothing conclusions are merited, but sometimes a less drastic finding would seem possible: a directed apology, or the correction of a departmental policy to prevent a future incident.

PUBLICATION OF SYSTEM

If the complaint procedure is to have its desired effect, it must be well publicized so that the entire community is aware of its existence. To accomplish this, the police must conduct a concerted program to inform the public of the procedures used by the law enforcement agency to review any complaints against it, and of the persons or other agencies to whom a complaint against the particular agency may be taken. This program should use all media available to it, the press, television interviews, its speaker's bureau, the schools, church groups, and in problem areas, a door-to-door campaign.

One method is to send a letter to the people of the community such as the following:

> To the People of the City of ......
>
> As Chief of Police, I wish to assure you that the Police Department is receptive to constructive criticism of the Department or valid complaints against its members. It has, however, been stated that for various reasons some persons are reluctant to go directly to the Police Department to register their complaints or criticisms. Additionally, others have said they do not know where to go in the Police Department or to whom they should talk regarding complaints.
>
> To assist you, the following information is set forth. My office is (*insert address*). If you wish to make a complaint, you may come to my office or phone (*insert telephone number*). You will be received by my (*insert name of officer or officers who will receive complaint*), whose job it is to investigate such matters. You will be treated courteously and all consideration will be given to the problem you present.
>
> However, if you do not wish to come to the Police Department, you may register your complaint in writing to me. Fill out the attached form and mail it in the addressed envelope which accompanies the form. As you will note, the envelope is marked "Personal and Confidential" so that it will be delivered directly to me.
>
> I hope that this will assist in assuring every person in the City that there is full opportunity to express opinion about the administration of the police department or to register a complaint against any of its members.
>
> Please feel free to express yourself about any legitimate problem which you think should be brought to my attention.
>
> (*Signed by Chief of Police*)

The form attached to the letter reads as follows:

> If you do not wish to appear at the Police Department, you may register your criticism or complaint by filling in this form and mailing it in the attached addressed envelope. Please write as much information as you can so that the Police Department can take appropriate action. It will be helpful if you give your name and address so that we may contact you for further information. Any information that you give will be kept confidential if you request it.

SIGN YOUR NAME AND WRITE YOUR ADDRESS
 AND TELEPHONE NUMBER HERE

WRITE THE DATE THIS FORM IS FILLED IN

WRITE THE DAY AND DATE OF INCIDENT OR ACTION

TIME OF INCIDENT OR ACTION

WHERE DID THE INCIDENT OR ACTION TAKE PLACE?

WRITE THE NAMES OF ANY WITNESSES,
 THEIR ADDRESSES AND TELEPHONE NUMBERS

IF A PERSON WAS ARRESTED, WRITE HIS NAME,
 ADDRESS AND TELEPHONE NUMBER

IF A POLICEMAN WAS INVOLVED, WRITE HIS NAME, BADGE NUMBER
 AND CAR NUMBER—IF YOU HAVE THIS INFORMATION

WRITE THE NATURE OF OPINION OR COMPLAINT
 (USE REVERSE SIDE IF MORE SPACE IS NEEDED):

COMPLAINT — METHOD OF MAKING

Any system adopted must assume that complainants will be given the opportunity to make their complaints in a dignified forum, should be appraised of the nature of the investigation, and should be notified of its outcome. Thus the first step in any such program is the establishment of an adequate complaint procedure. The normal police practice is to accept complaints by mail, phone, or in person—either at precinct stations or headquarters. The designation of either as a reception center for complaints answers the charge that that prospective complainants will be deterred by inconvenience or fear. It is often alleged on the one hand that a citizen is afraid to complain to his local precinct where the officer he desires to accuse may be assigned, while still others assert that the inconvenience of going to headquarters might discourage some citizens from complaining—particularly on minor matters—if that were the only place complaints could be lodged.

There is also the question of who can make the complaint. Such complaints might be lodged by superior officers, other officers, city officials and citizens. It is becoming common practice to allow anyone with a legitimate interest, including civil liberties organizations, to file complaints on behalf of aggrieved persons.

Many departments accept anonymous mail and telephone complaints even though it is generally believed that the sources of most anonymous complaints are unreliable. Since one of the first steps in a complaint investigation is normally an interrogation of the complainant who can often supply leads to other evidence, the investigation of anonymous complaints is handicapped from the start; but a department which refuses to investigate any anonymous complaint may be ignoring legitimate grievances. This possibility makes it unwise for a department to reject all anonymous complaints summarily, but it does not seem practical to require their full investigation where this diverts resources from the thorough investigation of complaints more likely to be well founded.

A workable compromise would be to accept all anonymous complaints, but to leave it to high-ranking officers, experienced in complaint investigation, to determine the extent to which they should be investigated. If the complaint procedure as a whole is conducted in an atmosphere of hospitality, any fear of complaining openly should diminish, and fewer valid complaints should have to be made anonymously.

Consideration must also be given to the form of the complaint. The department may require only a verbal complaint or may want it reduced to writing and signed by the complainant. The use of the latter course is justified as a means of preventing the complainant from changing his version of the facts. However, some citizens have been inhibited from filing complaints by warnings that the signed document may be used against them in a prosecution for filing false complaints.

The manner in which complaints are received is important, obviously. Police officers can discourage resort to the complaint procedure by receiving complaints in a grudging or hostile manner. Yet, at the same time, such action will react unfavorably by putting the whole system under a cloud of suspicion.

INVESTIGATION

The second step in any complaint system is the investigation.

The investigation should not be limited to whether or not an offense was committed and, if so, whether or not disciplinary action is necessary. Instead, the investigation should determine in what manner did the department contribute to the problem and how may it be eliminated or minimized in the future. An unfounded complaint often indicates that a greater effort to inform the public of law enforcement procedures or policies is necessary. A justifiable complaint either indicates that the department should reevaluate its current policies and procedures, whether they are concerned with employment requirements, attitudes, training, or basic local procedures, or it indicates a possible need for an evaluation, or reevaluation of the individual.

The normal investigation consists of interviews with the complainant, the accused and witnesses. A polygraph examination may also be conducted. The investigator's first duty is to contact the complainant. This is done for two reasons: to gather information, and to assure the person who has brought the accusation that his complaint is being acted upon.

The investigation may be conducted by the accused officer's unit commander, who conducts an investigation and reports his findings and recommendations to headquarters. One advantage of this system is that the familiarity of precinct personnel with the neighborhood where the alleged incident occurred is likely to facilitate the eliciting and evaluating of testimony. Placing the responsibility on lower-echelon personnel may heighten their awareness of the specific practices which evoke community opprobrium and of the particular officers in the unit who provoke complaints. The attack usually leveled against such a system is that precinct personnel and supervisors may have a great interest in covering up violations to shield their friends, to uphold the record of the precinct, or to conceal their own failings.

Another method is to have the investigation made at the division level by the officers' commander and the result reported to a supervisor who in turn checks the reports carefully to ascertain whether the investigating officer followed proper procedure for locating witnesses and other evidence and took complete statements. If he does not feel the investigation was complete, he can order a partial or total reinvestigation. After the supervisor is satisfied that a competent investigation has been conducted, he forwards the investigation report and his recommendations to the higher authority that decides whether to press charges against the accused.

It may also be provided that whenever either the investigating officer or the supervisor thinks it necessary, a hearing may be called as an aid to the investigation.

A third method is to establish a special division charged with responsibility for the internal integrity of the department. Its functions would approximate those of the military investigatory units that prepare cases for court martial proceedings. This division would have the responsibility of investigating and evaluating serious charges of misconduct made against police officers. Further, it would assume the investigation of personnel complaints when (1) personnel of more than one division are involved; (2) the personnel complaint or the investigation is of a nature that it would be impractical for the investigation to be conducted by the concerned commander; (3) sufficient supervisory personnel to conduct the investigation are not available at the division level; (4) adequate investigation facilities are not available at that level, and (5) when directed by the chief of police or requested by an officer of staff rank. Other charges can be investigated by the operating division themselves subject to review by the special division. If the division is not satisfied with the report, it can send the case back to precinct for further investigation or it can order a new investigation by its own personnel if necessary. As an additional deterrent to biased precinct investigation, the division could reinvestigate at random some cases initially referred to precinct.

Still another method is to establish a special unit which would investigate all complaints. Since an independent unit could devote its full time and attention to the investigation of complaints, it should develop familiarity with the problems involved and gain expertise in solving them. Also, the officers in an independent unit, being less often involved with the merits of a complaint than precinct officers, would tend to be more objective. Finally, the existence of a special investigating staff should convey to the community the impression that the police department gives serious attention to the processing of complaints. However, there are practical reasons why few departments rely entirely on special units. Every police department must have comprehensive criminal investigation machinery staffed with men trained and experienced in gathering facts and evidence. In most cases, it is simply easier and more economical to use this existing investigating capacity than to duplicate it with a corresponding apparatus used exclusively for the investigation of citizens' complaints. Furthermore, the advantages of a local unit investigation with higher echelon supervision are lost when a special investigating unit is exclusively used.

REPORT OF INVESTIGATION

The results of each investigation should be reduced to writing and compiled in report form for permanent retention. The report includes a summary of the complaint, pertinent portions of the statements of all persons involved in the incident, an evaluation of the complaint, and a statement justifying the conclusions reached as the result of the investigation by the internal affairs section. One or more of the following findings is also included in each completed investigative report:

UNFOUNDED. The investigation indicates that the act or acts complained of did not occur or failed to involve police personnel.

EXONERATED. Acts reported did occur but were justified, lawful and proper.

NOT SUSTAINED. Investigation fails to discover sufficient evidence to clearly prove or disprove the allegations made in the complaint.

SUSTAINED. The investigation disclosed sufficient evidence to clearly prove the allegation made in the complaint.

NOT INVOLVED. Investigation establishes that the individual named in the complaint was not involved in the alleged incident.

MINOR MATTERS

A person offended by minor police misconduct may desire

nothing more than an apology or the repair of property, and the facts of uncomplicated cases may be very easy to ascertain. In such instances, informal resolution can save the time and expense of investigation. If small problems can be resolved without investigation or legal proceedings, there is less danger of generating unnecessary friction among the parties concerned. It is possible, however, than an informal resolution can be used by precinct supervisors to cover up serious infractions and that precinct personnel may misinterpret departmental policy regarding what is justifiable conduct. To safeguard against this, an explanation and report of all minor complaints resolved by the accused's commander should be forwarded to the special complaint division or some superior designated by the chief for approval.

As an additional check on the implementation of department policy by precinct personnel, headquarters officials could, in all cases or in spot checks, follow up the settlement with a visit to the complainant to make sure he has received the relief promised him.

When there is reason to believe that some social action group or groups might have an interest in the particular complaint, that group should be contacted, and the facts given to the executive heads of the group, along with whatever determinations concerning these facts have been made to this point. They should be told that an investigation is being conducted. They should be told that they will be kept currently informed as the investigation progresses. If someone from an interested social action group has been assigned by that group to make an independent investigation, arrangements should be made, if possible, for the investigator and the police investigator to work together after each of them has had an opportunity to follow his own line of inquiry.

The person against whom the complaint has been made should be informed of the action that is being taken, in order that he, as well as everyone else concerned, will know that the department is engaged in an objective, fact-finding investigation. It allows the person against whom the complaint has been made an opportunity to supply information that may clarify the situation. It also emphasizes that the department considers this type of complaint to be one that requires its full attention.

Naturally, if the complaint is of such a nature that to inform the officer of it would frustrate the investigation, he should not be appraised of it. Such a situation would be the investigation of the officer's involvement in vice, gambling, or other criminal activities.

ADJUDICATION

The adjudicating body and the procedure followed can vary radically. Some complaint systems provide for no adversary hearing before a decision on discipline is reached. The reports are merely submitted to the designated official, usually the chief or sheriff, who makes the final decision on discipline.

While these systems have advantages in terms of low cost and time saving, it seems important that the parties and witnesses in a complaint proceeding have the opportunity to confront one another before the decision-maker. The confrontation should aid the trier in reaching a judgment on credibility and may result in the presentation of evidence and arguments that were overlooked in the investigation report.

The other method is to have some type of formal disciplinary hearing. In some instances it is held by the chief of police or some other official acting alone. Contrasted with this is the practice of having it conducted by a panel of officers, either permanently assigned or chosen on an *ad hoc* basis. The differences are inconsequential, the operation of the hearing being basically the same whatever form is used.

It is the better practice to have the hearing open to the public. Closed hearings may be felt necessary to protect the accused officer's reputation should the complaint prove unfounded. However, the main burst of publicity follows the incident or complaint, not the hearing; after a charge has been made, a public exoneration should be more effective than a private one. If the proceeding is open to the public, there is less reason for the complaint or the community to suspect that the department has something to hide. In most systems, the complainant is informed of the board's decisions and the reasons on which it was based. There is no danger involved in releasing this information to the complainant or to the public, and it can only serve to enhance the confidence of citizens in the fairness and objectivity of the hearing.

When corrective action is indicated by the finding, one or more of the following actions may be taken:

1. Counseling.
2. Training.
3. Oral reprimand.
4. Written reprimand.
5. Voluntary surrender of time off in lieu of other action.
6. Voluntary surrender of accumulated overtime in lieu of other action.
7. Demerits.
8. Suspension.
9. Fine.
10. Demotion.
11. Dismissal from the service.

NOTIFICATION OF RESULTS

The complainant and any interested groups must be notified of the results of the proceedings and the action taken. If dissatisfied, the complainant may protest the department's action to the commission on human relations, district attorney, grand jury, civil service commission, attorney general, city attorney, or the Federal Bureau of Investigation for their review. If the complainant has not already been furnished a listing of these other agencies or officials to whom he may complain if he is not satisfied with the results, it should be done at this time.

The news media and the community should also be informed of all corrective actions taken on complaints. If necessary, explain the policy reasons behind the particular methods chosen to correct the situation—dispel speculation in the matter.

When the finding of *sustained* is reached as the result of an investigation into a complaint of misconduct, an information form is placed in the personnel file of each police officer against whom such a finding is returned. Monthly and yearly reports should be completed and submitted to the chief of police and all departmental organizational units. The reports should contain a survey of activities and include information such as the types of complaints under investigation, the disposition of investigations undertaken, and the number of complaints registered.

POLICE REVIEW BOARDS

Numerous organizations have recommended the establishment of a police review board—a board independent of the police department which would review citizen complaints. The specter of a community filled with disciplinary boards, one for each of the various governmental functions, created for the purpose of protecting the citizen from improper bevahior on the part of governmental employees should strike fear into any reasonable man's heart since the basic concept is so violative of sound administrative concepts as to be untenable. However, the fallacy of the concept of civilian control of discipline is not so readily apparent at the present time because of the intimate linkage between the review-board concept and the civil rights movement.

Origin

The civilian review board idea originally was created to subvert the police. It is obvious that removing the police from the discipline and control of the city's elected representatives and making them subservient to a small group of private citizens creates a perfect setup for any subversive group desiring to infiltrate the review board and intimidate the police. Therefore, as a former national officer of the Communist party has pointed out, the whole idea of setting up civilian review boards was invented by the Communist party three decades ago. Their object, it is maintained, was to gain control of the police and paralyze them when riots and violence were instigated.

Erroneous Premises

The assumptions upon which the review-board concept rests,

when examined carefully, provide a rather sweeping indictment of the law enforcement group. Where any group attempts to step forward and divest the police executive of the responsibility and the authority for disciplining his force, that group is saying the following:

1. Police administrators and commanders are not capable of rendering impartial judgments in cases involving complaints against officers due to the fact that all police officers are imbued with a "pack instinct" which makes them shield the wrongdoer rather than search for the truth.

2. Law enforcement cannot qualify as a profession because of the inability of its practitioners to establish and to enforce standards of conduct among themselves.

3. The courts of the community, because of their close daily working relationship with the police, tend to share the tendency to protect the accused officer thus depriving the complaining citizen of an impartial hearing.

Enlightened citizens who share the professional police executive's desire to provide law enforcement services of the highest caliber are not likely to accept the politically expedient "solution" offered by review-board advocates. The problems of law enforcement manifested by citizens' complaints will not be cured or even revealed by a rigid legalistic hearing procedure or by a panel of citizen-judges concerned only with the immediate aspects of the specific case.

The external-board champions advance the argument that public confidence will be restored and maintained so long as the task of punishing the police is in their hands. It may be true that some citizens may take solace in the spectacle of punishment, but the community cannot hope to achieve a better level of police service simply by administering punishment. Negative discipline is only one minor aspect of police administration. The more fundamental facets such as recruitment, selection, training, supervision, direction and incentive are other parts of the overall process. Where misconduct becomes apparent, all of the basic processes by which the department is operated must be examined. Clearly this is the responsibility of the duly appointed and empowered public officials. The police or public safety commission, which is, in fact, a broad, policy-setting group, combines all of these diverse but related aspects of administration and thus becomes the responsible focal point of leadership. The review board, devoid of both responsibility and authority for the basic functions of administration, represents a superficial attempt to deal with more complex problems. Outside review boards represent a direct reflection upon inadequate police leadership since they can exist only where the police leaders fail, for whatever reason, to discharge adequately their responsibility to investigate impartially and deal with complaints by citizens against departmental personnel.

Review Board Is Not Needed

Those who champion the review board ignore the fact that elaborate legal machinery already exists for the channeling of complaints against the police. These include the police chief (who has more reason than anyone to ferret out any irregularities in his department), the civilian police commissioner (whose job was originally created to receive complaints from the public), the members of the city council, the mayor, the city attorney, the district attorney, United States Attorney General, the FBI, the grand jury and the Federal Grand Jury. All of these have remedial jurisdiction over charges of civil rights violations by police. Long ago it was claimed that local officials would cover up these violations, but no such excuse can be used today because, for several years, charges of police brutality have been within the jurisdiction of the FBI and subject to Federal prosecution.

Dilution of Authority

A citizens' board would dilute the responsibility of the police commissioner to maintain discipline of his department and result in a breakdown of morale among the policemen who have been doing their best in a dangerous and thankless job. The question of setting up such a board was carefully studied by the Royal Commission on the Police in Great Britain, who endorsed the principle that the administration of discipline should rest in the hands of the police chief. In its 1962 report it stated:

> The police are a disciplined body, and proper leadership requires that the administration of discipline should be in the hands of the chief constable. Any whittling down of this responsibility would weaken the chief constable's command of the force and this, again, would lead to a loss of morale and confidence. There is no strict analogy between a disciplined body like the police and the medical or legal professions, where it is proper that professional discipline should be administered by a specially appointed body rather than by a single individual. Moreover, a divided control over discipline could not easily avoid the danger of putting an accused constable in peril again after he had been tried and acquitted by his chief constable, and thus of infringing a basic principle of justice.

As the more specific issue of complaint review systems is examined, it must be borne in mind that the basic concepts of external control over the negative aspects of organizational control and discipline may well be applied in future years to every form of governmental endeavor. Thus, school teachers, judges, public health officers, nurses, district attorneys, public defenders, probation officers and the like may look to the day when the outside review system is employed in their field. Such must be the eventual outcome if the principles upon which external systems are based have validity.

Conducive to Intimidation and Destructive to Morale

These boards are conducive to the intimidation of police personnel. Because the power to discipline is the power to control, the civilian review board takes the police department out from under the people's elected representatives and places them under a politically oriented and often biased group of lay people who neither know nor understand police problems.

The establishment of a police review board, which would involve continual scrutiny of the police by an outside agency which has no responsibility for assuring effective police work but would be concerned only with criticism of the department, would adversely affect the morale and effectiveness of individual police officers. It is even possible that the police attitude may become "the only way to keep out of trouble is to do nothing."

This cannot be allowed to happen, for as Edmund Burke stated: "The only thing necessary to the triumph of evil is that good men do nothing."

Boards Have Failed

Probably the strongest argument against the board is the simple fact that where civilian review boards have been set up, they have failed to demonstrate their usefulness, or even reduce hostility to the police. They have failed to reduce community tensions, have provided a "sounding board" for dissident elements and for persons with a personal or political "ax to grind," and have confused and complicated governmental responsibility for the handling of police disciplinary matters.

SURVEY

In addition to receiving and investigating complaints, the police may conduct independent surveys to determine the impression created by the officer. A random selection is made from recently issued citations and an anonymous questionnaire is sent with a return addressed envelope. Inquiry is made concerning the demeanor of the citing officer, his appearance, attitude, courteousness, and helpfulness. The constructive or adverse comments of the citizens are solicited. All comments are evaluated and, if warranted, investigations or corrective actions are taken.

TRUTH SQUAD

More and more of late the police have been maliciously accused of brutality and malfeasance which the accusers have consistently failed to prove. The antipolice propagandists have relied upon the accusation alone to do the damage. Unfortunately, it does just that. The accusers often turn out to be the very people who are creating the climate of violence. Some of them have been proven to be the ones who initiated the violence. Then they have tried to blame the whole situation on the police. When the police have tried to defend themselves, these same people have accused the police of trying to cover up. It is all designed to deceive the public and divide the people from the police profession with a wall of hate.

This problem has reached the point where affirmative action must be taken to expose the falsity of the charge and the stupidity or depravity of the accuser. In such a battle, the police must use the strongest of all weapons, truth.

The falsity of the charges must be shown to the public and its confidence in the police reinforced. Every available means of education, information and public relations must be used. One of the most effective methods of accomplishing this is through the support of leaders of the community. These respected citizens are in a better position to impress the public with the truth than are the police, for they are disassociated from the conflict. Their impartial attitude will give weight to their views.

These citizens should be formed into a committee which is a cross section of the community, representative of all segments of society, respected by the people and completely beyond reproach. The committee should be completely independent of the police department even though a close liaison must be maintained for the purpose of getting needed information and avoiding anything which might embarrass the department.

The committee should be organized to investigate and prepare appropriate public statements and press releases. It should have a "truth squad" which is prepared and able to confront the agitator and reveal him for what he is.

It is surprising to discover how quickly an audience can be aroused against hate-laden polemics when a responsible citizen arises with sufficient facts to expose the propaganda of the opposition. Often the truth squad need do nothing more than use the Socratic technique of asking the propagandist what he means by "police brutality." Most of the time such reckless talk goes unchallenged. If the person claims to have proof of abusive police activity, then he should be asked if he has reported this to the chief, the city council, the mayor, the city attorney, the district attorney, the United States Attorney General, the FBI, or the local grand jury, all of which have remedial jurisdiction and can take direct action if there is a genuine basis for a complaint. In nearly all cases he will have failed to do so. If the speaker claims these agencies would only cover up for the police and the only remedy is to have a civilian police review board, then the truth squad must have the necessary information to expose the whole campaign for civilian review boards. The important thing is that citizens are willing to stand up to the demagogue and to tell the truth.

Chapter 9

ROLE OF THE INDIVIDUAL OFFICER

INTRODUCTION

T HE TRADITIONAL police officer stereotype of bygone years was a man everyone knew, loved and respected. He was the friend of people on his beat and an image of being helping, kindly and just. People had a chance to know him as a person in his walking of the beat. When there was difficulty and Officer "Clancy" needed assistance, the public would aid him because he was their friend and "People help their friends." Officer Clancy did a great deal of screening of delinquents through his personal knowledge of the young people, their families and activities. He knew the "bad" boys from the "mischievous" boys, when delinquency was recurring that would go unhandled unless he acted as the control, and when delinquent proneness was occurring that a stern lecture from "friend" Clancy could solve. Hence, two rival sandlot football teams settling their dispute momentarily would be pulled apart by the beat officer and sent home, instead of being taken to juvenile hall for disorderly conduct.

The officer on the beat acted as a delinquency prevention agent by knowing the parents who would take control measures when their youngsters were in danger of difficulty. Officer Clancy's image was enhanced by helping Mrs. Jones with her heavy bag of groceries, helping the small children across the street, and other good deeds.

The modern policeman is handicapped by his lack of public contacts which help him communicate a "helping" image to the public. Instead, his role implies one of trouble. People do not like trouble, and those with whom trouble or pain is associated as a role are rejected and become alienated in man's hedonistic demands. The modern, highly mobilized, police force can readily go anywhere there is trouble, but the policeman's public contacts become only those of trouble as he rides up in the police car with lights flashing. This efficiency of technology is devoid of warmth—to the public because there is little opportunity to see the policeman as a warm person, and to the policeman because in his occupation he must be geared to racing from one trouble spot to another. Under these circumstances, there is no opportunity for personalized communication to occur. The entire sequence of communication is impersonal.

This anonymity and isolation of the law enforcement officer must be broken down. The public's apathy toward law enforcement which is the product of that anonymity must be changed. The citizens must be actively on the side of law enforcement. The sort of passive tolerance that now seems to be the best that many communities can do by way of support will not suffice.

IMPORTANCE OF THE INDIVIDUAL OFFICER

The success of any enterprise is largely determined by its people, their individual competences, the values they hold and the quality of their leadership. It is equally true that the public relations of a force are affected by the conduct of every single officer on that force.

Every police officer, be he of Italian, Irish, Negro, Polish or other origin, by virtue of his uniform is a symbol of the law and represents the whole police department. Every act of an officer has meaning and significance beyond the individual. It has a consequence for every other man who wears the police uniform. It should be remembered that individual members of the community will generalize about the police department on the basis of their experience with each officer.

Indeed the police officer is more. He is the living embodiment of the law. He is literally law-in-action. He is the concrete distillation of the entire mighty history of the law. The meaning and value of the entire legal system are determined by the police officer's specific acts or omissions.

In a democratic society the conduct of the police officer

becomes the living expression of the values, meanings and potentialities of democracy. Democratic law is ethical law. It expresses and encourages equality and human dignity. The police are under the constant eyes of the public. To prevent discredit to himself and the department, every officer must perform his duties with dignity and decorum and extend equal courtesy and consideration to all people.

Being a police officer does not confer special privileges or immunities. It is an honorable and necessary occupation in the life of any community, but it does not endow you, as an officer, with the right to impose on other people your own personal ideas and opinions which are in conflict with existing law, nor does it give you the right in connection with your official duties to act with discrimination against any person or group of persons. The average citizen's respect for an officer depends upon the degree to which that officer impartially exercises his authority. This is especially true of the members of the minority groups, who may have little reason to respect an officer if it is apparent that they do not receive equal protection, courtesy and consideration from him.

Thus the most important factor, in building the right kind of image of the police force, indeed of our own way of life, is the policeman himself. He is the police department. He is the one who decides what the people in his city think about his police department. He is the only one who can do something about public relations. Why? Because he is the person who contacts the public, and the man who contacts the public is the most important link in any public relations program. Unless his relations with the public are good, smooth, friendly, and of a nature that produces continuous goodwill, most of the work of the chief and the public relations staff goes out of the window. The individual policeman is the fellow who decides and who determines the kind of relations his police department has with the public.

There is still another sound explanation for this. One of the most crucial factors in determining success or failure in a communication situation is the attitude of the receiver to the source, previous to and during the communication. It is for this reason that the quality of the relationship between the persons communicating is of far greater importance than the technical proficiency with which they communicate. We tend to believe people whom we consider to be trustworthy, regardless of what they say, while conversely we automatically disbelieve or discount the words of one whom we distrust. For this reason the typical member of the community will perceive a message offered by a policeman not only in light of the content itself but, more important, in the light of his previous attitude toward the police.

The place, then, to begin establishing more effective communication between police and community is not with the message that is to be communicated or even the system by which it will be communicated, but with the general image of the police in the community. Generally, communication channels ought to be as direct as possible. Often we place entirely too much emphasis on the mass media of communication, naively supposing that a favorable editorial will change the opinion of those who are hostile to us. This is typical, but not true. While the news media does provide the facts from which we make decisions and tends to reinforce us in the decisions we have made, it tends to be less effective when it comes to changing our attitudes from negative to positive or vice versa. Usually this is done by personal contact. Someone we know and trust offers advice or shares his attitude with us, and we find ourselves heavily influenced by it. The person who influences us in one field does not, of course, influence us in all fields; but if we analyze the basis of our own attitudes and opinions, we are likely to find a great deal of personal influence on them and relatively little of the mass media.

RESPONSIBILITY OF INDIVIDUAL OFFICER

Each officer must determine what he can do personally to enhance the image of law enforcement, for if a public relations program is to be effective, all members of the department must actively believe and participate in it. First and foremost, he must be capable of efficiency in his chosen profession. He must be technically and tactically proficient. He must know his job thoroughly. To achieve this, he must obtain a well-rounded police education from attendance at schools and through reading, research and study. He should seek out and foster associations with capable officers. At the same time he should observe and study their actions. He should broaden his knowledge through associations with members of other units and divisions, and keep abreast of current police developments. He must take every opportunity to prepare himself for the next highest job.

Yes, today's police work requires a man possessed of skills, training and information. Not only must he have these qualities, he must be recognized by others as having them. He must have the confidence and the skill which makes it possible for the rest of the community to say that what this man does is right and in the interest of the community.

BASIC PRINCIPLES

There are several basic principles that every police officer should understand and believe in if he is to be effective in the field of police community relations. They are as follows:

1. He must understand that there are many in our society whose opportunities have been limited because of economic and social factors.

2. His basic commitment must be a deep belief in the principle that all people are ethically equal, though personally and culturally different, if police programs and procedures are to further the cause of police-community relations.

3. Many persons are suspicious of the police because of early preconditioning by parents and others who may have advised them in terms of their own experiences and rumor. This may be changed by presenting a changing picture showing consideration, fair play and equal treatment for all.

4. The police must accept full responsibility for developing and carrying out a continuing program of police-community relations.

5. The police must be well informed on behavioral science as it relates to the many groups in the community.

6. They must know the changing community—its needs and expectations.

7. They must utilize community resources for cooperative planning to provide a solid foundation for the police-community relations program and procedures.

8. They must have not only rich consultive assistance, but experience and leadership within which is strong and vigorous, yet realistic and resourceful.

9. An effective police-community relations program will interrelate the needs and responsibilities of the individual police officer and the private citizen with the law enforcement complex of which both are a part in the community.

10. Each of them must stand for something and do something as an individual.

11. There must be interaction between all members of the department and the community.

12. There must be assistance, encouragement and in-service training of all police officers on a continuing basis in the police-community relations field.

13. The police must identify the need for supplementing regular police-community relations programs with special programs designed to better police-community relations in areas where such special programs are needed.

OFFICER MUST KNOW HIMSELF

The officer must also know himself and constantly strive for self-improvement. This requires constant self-analysis. The officer should fully evaluate his own attitude and disposition. He should consider his own weak points and shortcomings and ask himself the following questions: "Am I setting a good example for the citizens and my associates?" "Am I meeting the standards required of a good police officer?" "Am I proficient and do I possess the knowledge required of my position?" If the answer to any one of these questions is no, then self-improvement is urgently needed.

The officer should solicit the honest opinions of senior officers and supervisors about how he can improve himself. He can profit by studying the causes for success or failure of other officers, past and present. Such an analysis should recognize some of the emotional pitfalls of the profession that can and often do influence the officer's personality and his conduct with the public.

By nature, training, or experience, policemen are suspicious. Let us say or do nothing here to change that. Being suspicious helps to make one a good policeman. However, this highly desirable quality can be overdone and cause him to become suspicious of everything and everybody. This essential quality can make him unhappy and cynical. It is his suspicion that keeps him from trusting people. If he doesn't trust people, he can't very well like them. If he doesn't like people, his every contact with them is an unhappy one, not only for them, but for him. The whole problem is beautifully put in the following proverb: "Being suspicious may be no fault, but showing it is a great one." The policeman sees the results of the sins of commission and omission every day. He sees enough of this to warrant his being indignant and disgusted, to cause him to hate and to provoke an expression of anger. He becomes indignant, mad, disgusted. There is nothing wrong with him for feeling the way he does. Actually the things that kill and maim and hurt innocent people are the things he hates, but about the only way he can express this feeling is in terms of hate for the individuals who committed the offense that caused the accident.

If he understands what it is that causes him to get mad, he can avoid these emotional upsets and control himself. He will do a better job of handling himself and produce better results in this business of getting along with people.

Some citizens are predisposed to resent any approach by a police officer and are constantly looking for symptoms of "prejudice and unfairness." These persons will sometimes goad the officer into situations which will play on his emotions to the extent that he will react by allowing personal feelings to supersede his judgment. If the officer allows himself to become emotionally involved, his actions are almost certain to result in embarrassment to the citizen and discredit to the officer and the department. This is too heavy a price to pay for a moment's loss of dignity.

PERSONAL ATTITUDE AND CONDUCT

Do Not Be Unhappy

Since all the things that make any individual unhappy are part of a policeman's job, sooner or later most policemen begin to believe they should be unhappy. Add to this that an officer must be suspicious and negative, stand constant criticism, be discouraged more than he is encouraged, and be constantly on the defensive. These are enough to make any person unhappy. Add them up and we agree it takes a pretty solid person not to become a sad sack and a long-faced grouchy individual when he puts on the badge of a policeman.

If those things are not enough to make him sad, things he sees are—death, blood, hardships, moral misbehavior. All of these should make him unhappy. As a result, many policemen think there is no cause for them to be anything but unhappy. Yet, for every reason to be unhappy, there are literally hundreds of reasons to be happy. No other job offers so many opportunities to give service—to help his fellowman, to save lives and prevent injuries. No other job puts him into contact with so many people who are in trouble, who need help, who need somebody to talk to, who need a shoulder to lean on, who need a friend. There are other jobs, but they usually require him to sit in an office and wait for someone to phone or to visit and ask for help. In the police service, the officer doesn't wait for people to come and say, "I need you." He goes out looking for people in trouble and gives quick and immediate service. He seeks, and finds, and gives.

There is nothing so satisfying as serving one's fellowman. There is nothing that pays such big dividends to a man's soul. There is nothing that provides a more solid basis for continuing happiness. Happiness and success are parallel roads and as he grows older, a man finds that the joy of working to achieve is much stronger than the achievement itself. He finds that giving of oneself is the secret of unequaled happiness.

Unhappy people are not good salesmen, and unhappy policemen can never do a good, sound, productive, public relations job. Therefore, in order to get along with people, the officer must put a smile on his face and a song in his heart.

Let us now approach this self-analysis from a positive approach. Let us look for qualities of character and conduct that enhance the prestige of the individual officer and consequently favorably affect the entire department.

Faith in Self and Job

The officer must have faith in himself and in what he is doing. Many times he will have cause, serious cause, to question his own self on these points: "Are we doing any good?" "Are we moving in the right direction?" "Do people really appreciate what we are doing?"

Many times it will be necessary for him to reaffirm and restate his faith in himself and in his job because, if he is to do a good selling job, he must create faith in the mind of his public. He must provide them with a reason for having faith in him. When he builds this faith in the public mind, he is well on the road to giving the public a reason and a reminder to pay him what he is worth—in money—and in respect due a man who is true to his trust. He can't build this faith unless he has faith in himself. He must express that faith. It has been aptly said that enthusiasm is faith in action.

Pride

Pride has been defined as "having a sense of personal dignity and worth, having honorable self-respect. As we refer to pride here, we do not mean an undue sense of oversuperiority; neither do we mean conceit. Sometimes this "pride in the outfit" is called *esprit de corps,* or the common devotion of individuals to a group.

A policeman fails to do his part in the police public relations job if he does not have or fails to display pride in his department. A policeman has a right to be proud of being a policeman. The policeman should not feel that an apology or explanation is necessary for anything. The reputation of the police should be sufficient.

Morals

How a policeman conducts his private affairs is actually his own business. It becomes the business of his chief, however, if and when his affairs and conduct cause people to lose faith in him and other policemen. Then it becomes a matter of concern not only to his chief, but to his fellow officers because the public's faith in policemen is vital in the police public relations effort.

An officer is expected to set an example on or off duty for others to follow and must avoid behavior that tends to bring adverse criticism such as drinking to excess or gambling, engaging in loud arguments, use of foul language, and slovenly habits of personal hygiene. He must be extremely careful not to violate any law or regulation for which other people may be arrested. He must chose his off-duty associates and the places he visits with great care. Nothing is more damaging to the reputation of a police officer than his association with disreputable persons and his visiting places suspected or known to be disreputable. He must use great discretion in the exercise of his police authority while off duty in minor violations of the regulations, particularly in the neighborhood where he resides. Such off-duty activity and participation in neighborhood differences often creates deep resentment, and frequently results in complaints against the officer.

He should merit respect in his home life by adhering to a high moral standard, living within his means, taking precautions to see that his associates and the places he frequents are above reproach, maintaining cordial relations with his neighbors, and avoiding domestic quarrels. He must inspire confidence by taking care in his public life to avoid association with gangsters, gamblers and disreputable persons, to pay just debts and to avoid contracting unnecessary obligations, to be honest and aboveboard in all his dealings, and to avoid association with subversive organizations or groups advocating bigotry.

PHYSICAL APPEARANCE

The individual policeman becomes the mirror in which the police agency is reflected. The wise police official will insure that, to the maximum extent possible, the individual policeman creates favorable image in the public eye. How, then, is this favorable impression obtained?

Appearance

The uniformed policeman should present a neat and clean appearance when he greets the public. He, as a symbol of law and order in a free nation, a symbol of freedom from fear, has high standards set for him and the uniform he wears. His uniform should fit and be clean and neat. His brass should be well polished and his shoes shined. He should always be clean-shaven, his hair should be neat, and he should avoid extreme styles of haircut. His hands and nails should be in good condition. His gun, gunbelt and cartridges should be in perfect condition.

Having a wholesome appearance, wearing a clean uniform and operating with unquestionable behavior, will cause people to have confidence in him and his department and in the symbols his uniform and badge represent. Then his job becomes easier and more pleasant.

Bearing

Bearing reflects the individual police officer's confidence, professionalism and training. Improper bearing detracts from the favorable impression that could otherwise be created. When out on the street, he should stand erect and have a military bearing. He should walk properly so not to give the appearance of loafing. He should not lean on anything. He should not spit nor smoke on the street.

Attitude

A police officer must reflect a feeling and purpose of interest and assistance. A police officer who displays an attitude which denotes an overbearing demeanor will seriously damage a favorable police image.

Knowledge

All police, to be effective and efficient, must be well informed about the responsibilities of their office and of their mission. The individual police officer must have a thorough knowledge not only of police science but also of the society with which he deals. A police officer who is not professionally qualified in the basic skills of his field will not create a favorable public impression.

CONDUCT OF THE POLICE OFFICER

Conduct is an outward manifestation of character. People and the organizations they represent are judged on the basis of their conduct. It is a proven fact that many persons gain a lasting impression of all policemen based on the actions and attitude of the first officer with whom they come into contact. So, policemen must make good impressions—deliberately make good impressions.

In order to work effectively, the police officer must keep in mind the fact that his personal success depends upon the personal response of others to his various attitudes and approaches to police problems. The basic guide for the police in this field can be summed up in the three characteristics of tact, patience and courtesy. This is particularly important since about 90 per cent of his contacts are with good people.

While no simple set of "how-to" rules can be formulated which will fit all, or even most, human relations situations, a good general principle to keep in mind is the Golden Rule: ". . . whatsoever ye would that men should do to you, do ye even so to them"—to which we might add the corollary: taking into consideration their individual differences. Therefore, to apply this principle the officer will need to study people, and especially their differences, to be able to put himself in the other person's place.

The first step is to develop a genuine interest in people. The officer can discipline himself to like every person he contacts. He can do it by saying to himself, "I am going to like this person, I am going to make a friend here." Getting to know a person leads to an understanding of him within the framework of his human personality, with his weaknesses and his strong points. Out of such knowledge and understanding grows tolerance and even respect. Then the officer is beginning to be bigger than his experiences and his prejudices of the past. Then he will be a better policeman, a better salesman, and he will be doing a first-rate job of police public relations.

A police officer's job is dealing with people. Consequently, his initial approach must be made in such a manner that the citizen cannot interpret the officer's actions as anything but the just performance of duty in a fair, equal manner without prejudice or bias. Public respect and confidence is predicated on the officer's ability to create a favorable climate through impartial citizen contact. Where the essential elements of respect and confidence are lacking, the objectives of law enforcement are difficult, if not impossible, to achieve.

An officer stopping a citizen for any reason must bear in mind that most encounters will not result in an arrest. The ability of the officer to refrain from the use of words, expressions and attitudes that may offend will increase the chance for a favorable response from the citizen. Remember, initial attitude and approach will have a great bearing upon the effectiveness of the contact and will leave the citizen with a lasting impression of the quality of the officer and the entire department.

Policemen are in the criticizing business. An officer's entire official life is made up of a series of questions—questions for which he is seeking negative answers. He must look for things wrong, or he won't be a good policeman. However, he cannot let this keep him from being a good police salesman because, unless a policeman is very careful, he will soon find his life made up of a philosophy of, "What's wrong here?"

What can he do about this? He can start by promising himself he will look only for things that are right and things that are good, for a certain period each day. He looks for things to compliment rather than for things to criticize. As he is looking for things to compliment, he asks himself this question, "Is there something about me that causes me to have conflicts with people?"

He could say to himself while he shaves each morning, "I must not let looking for wrong officially cause me to look for it personally; I must remember that negative thinking can destroy my ability to sell myself and my fellow officers and the idea and ideals of policing to the public." One sure way to offset the influence of negative thinking is to say something nice about a few people every day. Try it for a month. Then if it works, keep on trying it.

A policeman has to say No may times a day. All of us should learn to say No pleasantly. It's very hard for a policeman to keep from sounding dogmatic, so softening his statements and softening his No will make him seem less dogmatic and will make him a better salesman.

Guidelines

The following are some suggestions which will aid the officer in his relationships with his fellow officers and with the public:

1. Be courteous and friendly.
2. Be dignified and confident in your ability.
3. Be sincere.
4. Be calm and maintain composure at all times both on and off the job.
5. Do not bluster or be overofficious.
6. Meet people easily and be tactful and considerate.
7. Maintain personal poise, show respect to your superior officers and individual members of the public.
8. Do not indulge in abusive oratory or display personal vindictiveness. You do not have to be hard-boiled to be a good officer. On the contrary, it indicates an inferiority complex, and a lack of confidence in your authority.
9. Maintain your person and uniform as well as possible.
10. Give assistance willingly and cheerfully.
11. Be exemplary in your conduct whether on or off duty. However, let us now emphasize that there is a distinct difference between service and servility, courtesy and softness, politeness and groveling.

COURTESY

Courtesy in police work is not only the mark of good breeding and gentlemanliness, but it is also a most practical asset in the performance of difficult and trying duties. What is courtesy? The dictionary defines it as "Genuine and habitual politeness, excellence of manners." Note the word "genuine." Thus, it must be real and sincere, and not manifested in hand shaking and back slapping or other superficial display in public contacts. It is also not softness or "playing the patsy," which begets only contempt, but, rather, it is a deep-rooted attitude which is manifested by good manners and consideration for others, which can inspire only admiration and respect. It is the sign of a he-man just as discourtesy, especially when coupled with authority, is the sign of a bully and a coward. You don't have to be "ornery" to be a good policeman, just as you don't have to use foul language to be forceful.

Police courtesy is built on the ability to show respect to others in both trivial and important contacts. By making a sincere effort to understand the other person's point of view, you acquire the key to understanding and good judgment in your police work.

There are many rules which serve as a guide for good manners and, consciously or otherwise, you follow certain principles of courtesy. Here are some general rules which have proved effective in cultivating police courtesy.

1. Do not make positive statements on a subject on which you are not well informed. When in doubt, keep silent.
2. Learn to take constructive criticism intelligently.
3. Look into the face of the person to whom you are speaking.
4. Ignore slight affronts of those with whom you come in contact unless they amount to insults.
5. Be strictly punctual for all appointments, both business and social.
6. Preface your request to see a driver's license by a brief explanation such as "Sir, you were exceeding the speed limit."
7. Maintain a military posture. Stand on your own two feet; don't lean against a post or wall, or drape yourself through the car window.
8. Refrain from making wisecracks or sharp retorts.
9. Do not talk about other people.
10. Never ridicule the mental or physical infirmities of people.

11. Remember that a pleasant facial expression is an asset. It is a smile (not a grin) that has been said to speak all languages.
12. Regard your brother officer as you do yourself.
13. Refrain from boasting.
14. Do not interrupt when another is speaking.
15. Guard against familiarity—be pleasant and courteous without becoming familiar.
16. Don't be afraid of the judicious use of the phrase "Thank you."
17. Maintain a respect for your uniform and loyalty to the honorable profession it represents.

SMILE

Smiling is a habit that is easily acquired. A smile can work wonders for the officer. It can stop a lot of criticism and can add much to police public relations. Adding a smile to every contact the officer makes will be effective for him and his department. A smile will whip fixed ideas. It will whip prejudice; it will whip old wives' tales. It will show people that policemen are pretty good fellows after all. It will show them that policemen are friendly.

Policemen are friendly—but being friendly is like being honest. A man must not only be honest—he must look honest. So, to protect and insure existing friendliness—smile. One's degree of friendliness is not measured by what he may say it is, or even what he thinks it is. It is measured by what other people think it is. A smile is one of the best police public relations tools a policeman has.

FLEXIBILITY

The police officer's attitude must be flexible at all times and must fit the situation. He deals with a multitude of differing personalities and differing police problems. It takes a flexible, easily adaptable person to be a good diplomat and salesman. It takes the same thing to make a good policeman.

No other job calls for the degree of flexibility that police work requires. The officer must be as delicate as a heart surgeon one moment and as rough as a roustabout the next. Yet, it can be done through constant and continuing self-discipline. He can make this quick change in himself regardless of where or what the assignment is and still maintain all the dignity of his job and his uniform. To do this he simply thinks about what he is doing, when and where he is doing it, and who is involved.

The police officer is a representative of the total community, and to properly discharge this obligation, the support of the populace whom he is sworn to protect must be maintained. This support cannot be realized if segments of the community believe prejudice is being practiced against them. The officer must continually evaluate his actions to insure that his approach to problems and contacts is professional and without bias.

A human approach is particularly mandatory, with every individual regarded as different from every other and every person treated as an individual. The contrary is a stereotyped approach which views the members of any groups as all alike and regards the various groups as superior or inferior to each other. An adequate understanding of the actual differences which exist between racial groups, which was discussed earlier, will greatly assist the individual officer in treating people as individuals rather than as members of a group.

If the individual merits of all persons handled by the police or with whom the police come in contact are weighed by the officer and any action taken suited to the circumstances of the incident, the stereotyped approach can be avoided.

VOICE AND WORDS

When a man speaks, his words convey his thought, and his tone conveys his mood. Much of the friction that occurs in daily life is attributable to a mere tone of voice.

Let us consider the following list of ways in which our spoken word affects us.

THE SPOKEN WORD

For Good Human Relations	*For Poor Human Relations*
Temperate language	Violent language
Charitable remarks	Gossip
Truth	Lies
Kind words	Sarcasm
Clean language	Obscene language
Well-modulated tone	Harsh language
	Profanity
	Boisterous speech
	Loud talk

The ability to speak sincerely, clearly and convincingly is truly the most important tool of the police. The chief fault is usually loudness. A low voice is always pleasing and can be cultivated. It should be low in pitch—not weak or timid. Such a tone of voice gives the impression of self-assurance and inspires respect.

Words are the police officer's stock in trade. The majority of his work situations involve little more than the use of words. Citations, field interviews and most arrests are accomplished through conversation. For each contact that requires the application of physical force or the use of a weapon, there are hundreds which are handled successfully by words alone.

The correct use of words will have a direct bearing upon the image which we project in practicing the art of good human relations. The public expects the police officer to be professional and therefore expects him to use accepted grammar when speaking, as well as an accepted manner of speaking.

Words convey ideas through meaning and inflection. Their impact is sometimes communicated more by the attitude and manner in which they are spoken than by definition. Words uttered by an officer who has allowed himself to become personally or emotionally involved frequently are spoken without thought of the reaction and often do not reflect the meaning intended by him.

It is important that officers realize the significance that is attached to language and actions if we are to avoid adverse public reaction. The term *police brutality* is generally thought to mean the unwarranted use of physical force. However, complaints of so-called police brutality are most frequently found to be complaints concerning offensive language or improper attitudes. Officers must strive to eliminate the public's use of the term *police brutality* by avoiding conduct which can be construed as police malpractice. Eliminating the use of offensive terminology or embarrassing language will assist in promoting a good public image and will foster a wholesome climate of cooperation in the community.

Use professional language in dealing with all people. Talking down to any person or group is immediately recognized and is not appreciated. Avoid the use of profanity, obscenities and colloquialisms used by teen-agers or criminal groups even when talking to such people!

The meaning of words is a reflection of personal experiences. In our large metropolitan centers there is a cross section of all walks of life with widely diversified religions, races and cultures, and each person is a product of influences present in his own environment. Many words and expressions accepted as proper and inoffensive within one group or geographical area have a degrading connotation when spoken in the presence of someone from a different group. Many words have no bad connotation by dictionary definition but have special significance when directed at certain persons or groups. Some officers may use such words in the mistaken belief that they are acceptable. For example, it may not be generally known that the words "Boy" and "Negress" when directed at a male Negro and female Negro, respectively, connote an inferior relationship in the case of the word "Boy," and immorality as to the word "Negress." Colloquialisms or slang used by officers should be avoided when speaking in the presence of individuals obviously from a different cultural background.

It is much worse to use a term that insults the group than to use one which insults the individual. It is, of course, desirable that no insulting terms of any kind be used, but terms which refer to a racial classification or a racial group should be most strenuously avoided. Officers must familiarize themselves with terms which are offensive to members of various minority groups and make certain they are never used in the performance of their duties or in the station. The wise officer will delete these terms from his vocabulary so that he is not inclined to slip when under stress.

It should not be too difficult for the police officer to realize that terms of derogation are usually met with resistance from the group to which they are directed. They create hostilities and tensions which can otherwise be avoided. Attitudes that develop from contacts wherein inappropriate language is used make the officer's job a more difficult one and give rise to the probability of a serious incident. It must be remembered that tensions build upon themselves, and each subsequent contact becomes increasingly difficult.

It is important to reailze that many terms which are used by minority-group members in reference to others within that group cause extreme resentment when spoken by an outsider, as the connotation becomes derogatory. This sensitivity is not restricted to ethnic minorities. For example, police officers find little significance in the term *cop* when the speaker is a member of the group. However, when used by a civilian, the word often assumes a different connotation and might be regarded as offensive regardless of the person's intention. Cop is a shortened nickname and as such is diminutive. When spoken contemptuously or in anger, the speaker's attitude overshadows the actual meaning of the word, with antagonism frequently the result.

Response in kind to verbal abuse directed at the officer will increase existing hostility and downgrade the officer in the mind of the person with whom he is dealing as well as with any others present. Attitude is an extremely important part of verbal communication. Facial expression, voice inflection and personal demeanor are as much a part of conversation as the words which are spoken. When coupled with words, an improper attitude can be devastating. Acceptable words when accompanied by such an attitude can create the impression that, "Your actions speak so loudly I can't hear what you say." How many times we have heard the statement by an angered citizen, "It's not what he said, but the way he said it," all the while admitting the validity of the citation. Harsh verbal contact without modifying facial expression is interpreted wrongly as hostility, and will in turn generate hostility in the listener.

Officers whose voices are loud or harsh must be doubly careful in all their vocal contacts, especially on the telephone.

OVERFAMILIARITY

All contacts by police officers in the performance of their duties are business relationships and should be conducted as such. The person who is the object of the police contact is very likely in an agitated state and will often interpret any tendency toward familiarity on the officer's part as a serious breach of professional conduct.

The use of first names or personal remarks is no more appropriate in a police contact than it would be in any other business transaction. Common courtesy dictates that first names in reference to adults should never be used. This familiarity is a privilege reserved for close acquaintance. The use of first names assumes magnified importance within minority groups because this tends to be belittling. Moreover, it is a breach of common courtesy.

TICKETS

Most policemen could do a much better job of preparing people for bad news. When an officer issues a traffic ticket, it is just another job in a long and tiresome day; but to the man who gets the ticket, it is an occurrence he will talk about for years. How the officer handles him is very important to the officer and to his department.

While the experience is routine for the officer, the citizen is undergoing quite a different feeling. He may be frightened, abashed, angry, or a combination of these.

The officer must take the time, he must make the effort. He must learn the talent of breaking the news gently. He must be cool, courteous and firm. He should explain to the citizen the reason for his action. He should not enter into any arguments over the merits of the case, rather he should inform the citizen he has a right to a hearing before the court. The officer must make him understand that the arrest is not a thing between the two as individuals, but an official matter which the officer has to do regardless of how much he dislikes it. The officer should always give him time to brace himself for the shock. He should prepare him for the test of "overloads" to his personal dignity.

It is such a common occurrence for a policeman to issue a traffic ticket, serve a warrant, or to make an arrest that he fails to realize what he is doing to the person's emotional balance and his ego. Policemen are not agreed that they could successfully use a "canned" approach to people, but there should be no disagreement on this point. When a man faces an unknown situation, he goes on the defensive. His body processes prepare him for battle.

In the conversation with his customer, the sooner the officer clarifies what he is going to do, and the sooner he gets over to the customer that here is a friendly policeman, so it can't be too bad, the quicker the customer's glands will signal the "all clear" and thus provide him with at least an even break on breaking the bad news.

It will be less of an ordeal for all concerned if the officer acts in a businesslike yet considerate and courteous manner. He should never apologize for serving the citation, ticket or summons (I'm sorry. Sorry, mister, but this is my job), but he should attempt to explain the seriousness of the situation and the necessity for exercising control. When dealing with minor offenses, he can explain what the offender did wrong. If it is a technical violation, he can explain briefly how it could have been avoided, or in instances of unsafe or improperly equipped vehicles, explain to the offender the legal procedures to be followed upon correction of the defect.

If the officer issues a citation, he should inquire if the person is familiar with the citation procedures and explain that the person's signature is not an admission of guilt but merely a promise to appear in court on the date stated. Although this approach may seem somewhat repetitious of what would be considered common public knowledge, it has been discovered that many persons do not understand the procedure. Thus, the expenditure of a little time and courtesy may avoid confusion while presenting an image of the "helpful" law enforcement officer. Further consideration must be given to specific types of contact between the police and the public.

INQUIRIES

Persons seeking information should be courteously informed. Never give misinformation. If you are uncertain, try to find out from some other source. Do not be afraid to say "I'm not sure, but I'll try to find out."

Give information in a spirit of cheerful willingness and with a desire to be helpful. It will only take a moment to check a map for a motorist or to look up information. If the information is not immediately available, it can usually be obtained by telephone.

Inquiries by telephone should be treated in the same manner as though made in person. A life may depend upon the promptness and efficiency with which a telephone is answered.

Many times police officers are approached by citizens with a problem which is not a police matter. In such cases the officer should be patient, friendly, pleasant, and as helpful as possible by advising the citizen where to turn for the solution of his problem.

CRIMINAL COMPLAINTS

Many complaints are brought to police attention by complainants who come directly to the office of a law enforcement agency. When this happens, the complainant usually has a personal interest in the case. For this reason he is generally ready and willing to furnish all the information since his complaint very likely involves either his personal property or money or that of someone related to him.

Many complainants are nervous and somewhat bewildered when they come to a police station, and any inconsiderate treatment of them will only add to their confusion. The impression they receive is often a lasting one. Being a complainant is far from an everyday experience for the average citizen, and he will generally remember for a long time exactly what occurred during the interview. The officer interviewing such a complainant is in a position either to make a lasting friend by treating him courteously, or to make an enemy by any discourteous treatment. Even though the contact is on an individual basis, the impression which this citizen receives from this one officer may affect his entire outlook towards law enforcement.

The officer should respect the complainant and treat his complaint as though it were important, even if it is trivial. It is not trivial to him! A lack of interest in his story is a breach of common courtesy. The officer must show a sympathetic interest.

If the officer is sympathetic in his attitude and considerate in his choice of words in his face-to-face dealings with the complainants, it will do much toward easing the anxiety of the complainant and gaining his good will.

Complaints should not be unnecessarily detailed. If referral to another command is necessary, refer the complaint not the complainant.

Many times a private citizen will approach an officer who is on duty and make a personal complaint. These complaints may be of a minor nature and are frequently made by women. If an officer receives and investigates a complaint made by a woman, the conversation he has with her and the manner in which he questions her is likely to produce a lasting impression, good or bad. This impression may expand, because the woman will probably relate the incident to her friends, generally voicing her opinion as to whether or not the officer who interviewed her was intelligent and businesslike or otherwise. Public opinion of law enforcement officers is often molded in this manner, and an officer cannot afford to risk a bad impression even in casual contact.

When an officer receives a complaint while off duty, it is usually of a serious or personal nature. An officer has to be very careful in handling this type of complaint. Under no circumstances should the officer handle the complaint by himself if a member of his family is involved. If he does so, he places himself and his department in a very difficult situation. If the complaint is not of a personal nature, the officer should give it his immediate attention, guided by the rules and regulations of his department. If it is impossible for the officer to handle the complaint himself, he should direct the complainant to the proper agency, making the initial contact himself. The personal contact which an officer makes on and off the job is very important, and a little extra effort on his part will be of great benefit to all of law enforcement.

Another source of complaints is by letter. Most of these complaints are directed to administrators of an agency, but sometimes an officer of a lower echelon will receive them. They should be answered promptly regardless of merit, for the officer often develops a contact which will be useful to him in the future. Such letters should never be merely reviewed and filed because an officer or administrator subjects his department to criticism by failure to answer complaint letters promptly.

Consideration of Complainant

Many people have a poor opinion of public servants. They may even expect to be insulted although in recent years this attitude has been gradually changing for the better. The outmoded idea that police officers must act "tough" may have stemmed from a narrower jurisdiction in earlier years which confined police work more exclusively to criminal matters. Today the increase in the flow of traffic and the liaison between the police and the public in other related matters has helped to change the picture. An officer must remember that a complainant has a personal interest in a case. He usually has information to divulge to an officer, but the officer's attitude may cause him to change his mind. In many cases, the complainant at the time of first contact with the police has not made up his mind completely as to how much information he will divulge. The person is sometimes nervous and bewildered, and to insult him would further confuse him. Usually this face-to-face experience is a big event in the complainant's life even though, to the officer, the complaint is unimportant and commanplace. Thus, the demeanor of the officer is a crucial factor in this relationship.

Courtesy Toward Complainant

If courtesy is shown toward the complainant, the officer can become a friend of the complainant for life. Many times an officer limits the extent of his courtesy to only those who are influential. Perhaps a department cannot do anything about the complaint for the complainant, but the courtesy of attentiveness is still desirable. Often in such circumstances that is all the complainant is seeking. Many times nothing concrete can be done except to show kindness and notify him of possible future developments. An officer should be patient, civil, attentive, businesslike and clear in conversation. He should never be curt, surly, gruff, inattentive, casual, sarcastic, or argumentative. It is usually better for the officer to hold his peace, even in the face of unfair criticism of himself and his department, than to become involved in an argument.

Interviewing Complainants — Personal Calls

When it comes time to interview a complainant, the officer must remember that a great deal more can be accomplished in privacy. The person being interviewed should be made as comfortable as possible. Generally it is better to let him talk, if he wishes, about things not related to the main topic of conversation, as this approach will usually help to win his confidence. The interviewer should not flash notebook and pen right away as it may have a negative effect on the complainant and cause him to freeze. He should be allowed to talk first and be given a full opportunity to tell his story. The interviewer should have him repeat the story since a second account will give the officer an opportunity to check the story for authenticity as well as to make notes. Furthermore, such a review helps to organize thoughts and will make the interview more productive.

Each interview should be as thorough as possible since it may be the only chance to gain information by this means. Before the complainant leaves, the officer should know, at a minimum, full name and any alias of the complainant, his address, place of employment and residential and business phone numbers. An officer might consider this person as a future confidential informant, or he may find this information vital when it is decided whether or not a law had been violated and whether a legal arrest can be made. This is a decision which the officer must make himself, or he can consult his superior officers for their decision. Before the complainant leaves, however, the officer should assure him that something of an affirmative nature will be done; or if this is impossible, he should be told why no action can be taken.

Psychopathic Complainant

The officer may be faced with a complainant who is mentally disturbed. This situation calls for the greatest amount of tact and patience. The officer should try to listen attentively to detect, if possible, the purpose of the person making the complaint. An argument will rarely do any good, and even if the complaint appears to be groundless, the officer should make a record of it so further complaints from this source may be evaluated properly.

Complaints in Regard to Automobile Thefts

Auto thefts constitute a major source of concern to peace officers. If an auto theft complainant appears in person, much of the confusion which often arises can be avoided. Sometimes an officer's suspicion may be aroused as the complainant might, for example, be trying to hide a hit-and-run accident or the use of the car in the commission of a crime. If such suspicions exist, the officer might prepare a written statement in which the complainant agrees to prosecute the perpetrator of the theft if he is apprehended. Never take as final the word of a person who telephones a stolen-car complaint. The owner of a car alleged to have been stolen should be contacted in person to make sure the complaint is authentic. Likewise, when a stolen car is recovered, the owner should be notified in person.

TELEPHONE PROCEDURE

The citizen's first contact with the police department is often a telephone conversation with an officer. On the telephone the officer is the police department's voice and whatever he says and how he says it creates for the citizen an impression of the department. The tone of voice is important. He is speaking to a person, not a telephone device. Every time he picks up the phone, he is doing a public relations job. It may be good, bad, or indifferent. He should always try to do the good public relations job.

When considering proper procedures for the use of the telephone, courtesy and consideration are always the keywords. Even when receiving calls from persons who are agitated or excited, the proper action remains much the same as in normal telephone calls. Since a large part of police telephone work is receiving calls, the following procedures are essential ones:

1. Answer promptly. Nothing is more exasperating than to be left on the other end waiting for your answer.

2. Identify yourself immediately after answering.

3. Speak courteously, clearly and directly into the mouthpiece, avoid gruffness or curtness at all costs.

4. Have pad and pencil handy. Make notes when necessary. Do not make the other party wait while you secure same.

5. Pay attention to what is being said. It is annoying to have to repeat messages simply because you have not given the conversation your undivided attention. If the call is for assistance and it warrants it, the caller should be given a realistic time estimation of when the call will be answered. If the assistance will be placed on a "hold" status until a unit as available, the person should be told so, and why. This simple act of courtesy may help to alleviate the expectancy and impatience of the caller. When the complaint is one which is not handled by the particular agency, or a response is not warranted, the caller should be given a brief explanation as to why the agency does not handle such matters, and if possible a reference should be made to the agency which does. In emergency situations it might be better to have the telephone call transferred to the appropriate agency. Again, the courteous, sympathetic approach in handling telephone calls is of more importance than is usually realized.

When the officer makes a call, he should follow the same basic guides of courtesy and consideration. They may be stated as follows:

1. Have in mind what he wishes to know or say when his call is answered.
2. Identify himself and state his business.
3. Have pad and pencil available. Make notes when necessary. Proper procedures can result in good telephone usage and are important to proper police work.

PERSONAL CONTACT

Mounting men in cars and doing away with the foot patrolman have greatly decreased the policeman's contact with the public. That is not good.

There is much that can be done about it. The average policeman in uniform, in a police car, is not busy on calls all the time. He can get out of his car. He can walk into the corner drugstore, service station, lumberyard, or men's clothing store. He can talk to three or four people in these places while his partner stays in the car. He may see a man washing his car or mowing his lawn. He can get out and talk to him. "But," he may ask, "what'll I talk to him about?" He has the finest speech in the world all ready. He sticks out his hand and says, "I'm John Smith, your policeman in this district on the evening shift. I just wanted to stop by and get acquainted with you and to let you know we are available to you for service. Any way we can be of help, let us know." This plan works.

The officer must get down among the people. He should call on three or four citizens every day. Such action will do much good for the officer and his department.

TAKING CRITICISM

The citizen has always criticized his public employees and probably always will. There are two reasons for this. One is that the citizen pays the salaries of his public servants. The second is that when he criticizes his police, he is given a feeling of importance. It makes him feel that he is not dominated, enhances his self-esteem and helps to maintain his self-respect.

However, as some policemen handle this criticism, it becomes a top hazard and a real liability in the police public relations field. It need not be. It must not be detrimental. Listening to citizens criticize can be a good public relations tool. It can become a real sales asset. Many successful police officers and police administrators have said they find listening to gripes and complaints is not offensive when you discount it; on the contrary, they say they find it rather interesting. It is known that the criticism and complaints about policemen must be discounted because people are prone to stretch a bit those things which they present as facts when they talk about their operation, their accident, their arrest, or their contact with the police.

Criticism is part of the police job, as it is a part of any job. So, rather than beef about it, the officer must accept it as such. Getting wet, getting cold, getting blood on his hands—these are all part of the police job. He is accustomed to these and more. He must also get accustomed to being criticized. If it gets in his hair and he can't take it, he should admit he has made a mistake, turn in his badge and find some job where he won't be criticized.

A top police administrator once said, "Show me a policeman who never gets criticism, who never gets a complaint filed against him, and I'll show you a man who is not doing very much." Successful and productive policemen catch hell every day. As long as a man is a policeman and really working at the job, he will be criticized. The higher up the ladder he climbs, the more criticism he will get. So, when some citizen wants to gripe, he should let him gripe. He is trying to tell the police something. True, he may get it all confused. He may be a little rude. He may be a little rough, but if the officer maintains a level of self-control, he can sift out all the rough points and get from the citizen the message he is trying to give. He is trying to tell something about the police service. The officer should not argue with him, rather he should listen and learn, to improve the police service.

The officer should not underestimate the difficulty of listening. To meet this, he must be prepared for it. If he can learn to take criticism in a pleasant, agreeable manner, and most certainly he can learn to do this, he will be very proud of that developed ability, and his added qualification as a well-trained police officer.

Handling of Dishonest Cop

The smart policeman, and the one who is wise, will defend his fellow officer as long as that officer is in the right. He must never defend an action of a policeman who is crooked. On the contrary, he must do all he can to get that crooked officer out of police service. The faster the honest policemen help their chief clean house of the few undesirables they may have in their department, the sooner they will be on the road to better police public relations.

POSITIVE INDIVIDUAL ACTION

It has often been said that the police officer is stereotyped. All that people see is the badge, the gun and the stick. They do not see the man behind the badge, nor the human qualities of compassion or understanding. The man is "invisible," but with concentrated efforts to humanize the police, this can be changed. To overcome this problem, it is up to each officer to get to know the people he serves. When people know an officer, they can defend him from unfair attacks by others; they will have confidence in his judgment and they can cooperate with him.

In order to combat the impersonal barrier which exists between officers and citizens, some departments have sent patrolmen on a door-to-door canvass of various neighborhoods. The officers contact individual residents, and introduce themselves. The officers may pass out cards giving the residents emergency numbers which they may call when they need assistance. In other cases, the officers ask the citizens how the department can provide better service to the area and whether there are particular problems presently existing which the department should investigate. The officers might invite the individuals to attend a police-sponsored function or meeting. Besides a house-to-house canvass, the officers could contact the proprietors of businesses where the people might congregate and also attempt to contact the individuals who frequent these places. These might include barbershops, beauty salons, pool halls, bars, bowling alleys and other such congregating places.

Not all of these attempts to meet the citizens on a friendly basis will be successful; not all will be fruitful and directly lead to the improvement of attitudes. The officer should be prepared to accept hostility but then should attempt to break through the barrier. Often this hostility is based on the community's wrong impressions. These contacts permit the officer to refute, by words and action, unfair or distorted charges and thereby eliminate misconceptions regarding police conduct. This is not an easy task, but the ultimate goal is worth the patience, understanding and effort.

Chapter 10

POLICE AND THE PUBLIC

INTRODUCTION

The police officer alone cannot solve all the problems of police and community relations. All citizens have a role to play. The police officer has an important position on the team, but it must be a team on which the churches, schools, civic leaders, and newspapers have a position to play also. However, so that the police officer can properly and effectively play his position, he must establish and maintain friendly relations with all other members of the team, so that community problems can be discussed with mutual confidence and respect, and without reservation.

ROLE OF THE CITIZEN

The public too often fails to realize that it must play a part in law enforcement. Its role must be active rather than passive, constructive rather than irresponsibly critical, cooperative rather than negative. The time has come when the people can no longer ignore their responsibility and the vital stake they have in improving and supporting the forces of law and order. People want to help, they want to do their part, they want to be good citizens. They want the very best law enforcement. Consequently, they will participate in any program that is contructive and to their own betterment and will help maintain their family and neighborhood. Unfortunately, society as a whole is relatively apathetic to law enforcement except and until it becomes involved, either as a crime victim or a traffic violator. In either circumstance, people are not receptive to the problems that confront law enforcement. Thus, in the last analysis, the brunt of the load must be borne by the police. This means that a definite plan of action with well-defined policies must be established.

PERSONALIZE THE POLICE

In formulating such a program, it must be always remembered that effective law enforcement is the foundation of all good public relations, but it is not enough. The performance must be told about, understood and appreciated. This is a story that does not tell itself. We must drive home our message that the vast majority of men in the police and law enforcement professions are honest and devoted public servants, dedicated only to the public welfare.

It must also be brought out that a policeman, too, is a human being. To many people the officer is an impersonal symbol of the power of society. Too many see just the badge, gun and night stick, rather than the man behind such tangible symbols of authority. To many citizens, the man is invisible. He should not be fitted into a convenient stereotype. He is an ordinary guy from any and all of the various backgrounds of the hundreds of national, religious and ethnic groups which make up this wonderful nation. He is just like the rest of society, yet with one vast difference. When he takes the oath of office and is trained for duty and equipped with shield, uniform and revolver, he becomes a different man, a man apart. He is no longer an ordinary citizen; he is a representative of government; he is an arm of the law, and the legal powers that we have given him are tremendous and awesome. No one realizes the extent of these powers and their implications more than the conscientious policeman, and even more importantly from the public viewpoint, the modern, professional and conscientious police administrator.

The public must learn the true role of the peace officer in our society. Many people, if not most people, do not understand the complex role that the policeman plays in society today. Most people, through personal contact as well as movies and television, know of the traditional strictly law enforcement functions of the police.

The other aspects of twentieth century police work must

be shown. The positive aspects of crime prevention and also the protection of society must be emphasized to the community as a whole.

OBJECTIVES AND GENERAL GOALS

The first step in such a program is to outline the objectives and general goals. Such goals will include the following.

1. To foster and improve communication. To interest citizens in law enforcement activities and acquaint them with the jurisdiction, responsibilities and services of the police agency, and, hopefully, to foster mutual understanding in the relationship of the police and the total community.
2. To portray adequately law enforcement as an integral part of the community. To inform the public that the police are its friends and its representatives.
3. To encourage the public to cooperate and assume responsibility for law and order. To lend stress to the principle that the administration of criminal justice, in all its ramifications, is a total community responsibility.
4. To develop public understanding concerning police problems.
5. To establish clearly the need for the performance of police tasks and make them easier.
6. To create an atmosphere for community pride and respect for its police agency.
7. To foster and increase police professionalism through pride and satisfaction in the performance of duties. To make the officer realize that he is working for the community and is not a free agent enforcing the law as an individual.
8. To assist in attracting better recruits for law enforcement.
9. To promote interprofessional (teamwork) approaches to the solution of community problems.
10. To enhance cooperation in the relationship of police with prosecution, the courts and corrections.
11. To assist police and other community leaders in an understanding of the nature and causes of complex problems in people-to-people relations, thereby to encourage intelligent and prudent handling of these problems.

Thus an effective community relations program is one that does the following:

1. Promotes better understanding and an attitude of respect between the members of the department and those in the community.
2. Enables the residents of the community to understand the difficulties facing the department and how they as citizens can help to overcome them.
3. Encourages all residents in the community to be law-abiding and cooperate with the entire law enforcement complex, thus assuming a greater responsibility in this particular phase of community affairs.
4. Maintains a bridge of communication and a joint effort between the many public and private agencies and individual groups to deal with specific aspects of the total police-community relations program.
5. Emphasizes crime prevention rather than apprehension or rehabilitation. The most promising area of progress in crime preventions is in the field of predelinquency; therefore, special emphasis should be placed at the predelinquency level.

COMMUNITY RELATIONS SECTION

An effective community relations program envisions a myriad of activities to promote the image of the police through the use of expanded personal contacts in coordination with the traditional methods of public relations. The complexities of such an overall program necessitates strict coordination in order to gain the full benefit of the efforts expended. To accomplish this, it has proven beneficial to establish a community relations section. It should report directly to the head of the agency.

It should be headed by a ranking officer. All permanent staff members of the community relations section should be carefully chosen with consideration being given to interest, temperament, experience, tactfulness, common sense, lack of prejudice, speaking ability, appearances and character. To broaden the public relations base of the department, a policy could be followed of rotating members of the force through the program as assistants.

The function of the community relations section is to co-ordinate, initiate, evaluate, and also act in an advisory capacity for programs which may affect police-community relations.

The basic responsibility of this section is to establish communication with groups and organizations. It should always be available to anyone who evidences an interest in law enforcement. Thus this section will give classroom lectures to school children, appear before religious, civic, business and veterans groups and participate in discussions on radio and television. The officers will also conduct tours through local police facilities for interested residents of the community.

It would be the function of the public relations unit to constantly remind patrolmen and all other personnel in the police organization of their unavoidable roles as public relations agents, and one of the chief tasks of the unit would be to convince law officers that public attitudes, in fact, help or hinder the police purpose. Unfortunately, there is often little that can be done to eliminate undesirable behavior among line personnel, short of the usual sanctions of reprimand, suspension and dismissal. Because the patrolmen can sabotage a public relations program merely by failing to be courteous, deviations which so often hurt the departmental image are not always amenable to formal sanctions. It is apparent that the public relations staff in this case will have to rely upon the persuasion of example and carefully worded memoranda to achieve desired results, since the behavior of the law officer is so very dependent on personal inclination and individual morale. The formal sanctions mentioned above might be extended to cover less errant, but nevertheless damaging, patrolman behavior, but this decision and its enforcement should be the prerogative of the police commissioner.

Members of the unit should be especially capable of recognizing undesirable behavior patterns before irreparable damage is done to the public's opinion of the police department. It is suggested that monthly or at least bimonthly meetings be held with commanding officers to discuss special problems of morale and performance and to arrive at solutions to them. The very fact of the meetings should help to promote a better public relations consciousness throughout the entire police organization.

Improvement of Public Relations Training

The public relations staff should also work closely with the police academy to incorporate public relations material into every training course which is even remotely concerned with the creation of favorable citizen attitudes. If the recruit can learn to associate the value of good public relations with all phases of police work, the difficulties of errant behavior and performance mentioned above would be greatly reduced. The public relations staff must also conduct refresher seminars for in-service policemen, so that a much needed preoccupation with citizen opinion could permeate the entire department.

Improvement of the Measurement Function

The existence of a permanent public relations unit will also facilitate the development of special techniques for measuring public sentiment and evaluating the effects of police public relations efforts. It is recommended that all letters either praising or condemning the department be channeled to the public relations staff where the correspondence can be recorded and analyzed. Telephone calls can be routed from the office of the police commissioner, the lobby desk, and from all other parts of the headquarters building if a caller wishes to voice a complaint, ask a question, or express his thanks concerning some aspect of police service. The time and effort saved the rest of the department would be substantial, and the proposed centralization of this type of communications would enable the police to feel the pulse of public opinion better. It would replace the relatively haphazard system of receiving messages from the public and would allow for the observation of trends in changing citizen attitudes. Evaluative reports made of incoming correspondence and telephone calls will definitely aid the police commissioner in his policy decisions. The concentration of the communications function would also make for flexibility, as the commissioner would be able to change the tone and scope of the public relations program at a moment's notice.

The public relations unit would assume special responsibility for expressing departmental appreciation for citizen aid in routine and emergency situations. It would publicize the fact of such aid whenever public relations would be enhanced by the information. The unit might establish an official program of citizen commendations to parallel the commendation system within the police organization itself, and in all cases would emphasize personal contact with the residents of the area. Patrolmen and other line personnel would aid the public relations staff by reporting the individuals and groups which should receive a note of thanks from the department.

FACE-TO-FACE COMMUNICATIONS

Face-to-face communications include rallies, speeches, door-to-door "salesmanship," agitation—in short, the range of activities in which people communicate verbally in direct face-to-face situations.

The Message

To be effective, the message must get a hearing, be understood and bring about the desired response. To accomplish this, the message must attract attention. Its meaning must be gotten across. This can be done by presenting it in terms the group will understand. It must be so organized as to arouse personality needs in the crowd which will be favorable to the police. The action urged must be such that it can occur. Further, that action should be important to the members of the crowd.

To be effective, the peace officer must know in specific terms what he desires to say, how it should be said, to whom it should be directed, and where and when to say it. These principles are essentially those which apply to all types of propaganda and their dissemination.

Specifically, the officer must be certain of the message he wishes to convey. That message may be cooperation with the police or developing interest in a positive national and community program. While actual phraseology should not be so planned that the advantages of apparent spontaneity are lost, the theme or line of persuasion can be purposefully preplanned and the questions anticipated.

Presenting the Message

The manner of presentation is of paramount importance. As in any method for propaganda dissemination, the message must be understood. Explanation of themes must be in terms which the individual addressed understands; he must be able to relate what is said to him in terms of his own experience, not the officer's. To present the message effectively, the officer must understand his audience thoroughly. He must have empathy—thoroughly be the other person. Certain "rules" assist the officer in achieving this sense of identification:

1. Carefully avoid an appearance of dogmatism in belief when dealing with a hostile person.
2. Stress what areas of agreement exist between the police and the audience.
3. Strive to keep the attention of the audience away from minor points of difference.
4. Work toward a predetermined conclusion but by means of the audience's method of reasoning.

Selecting the Audience

In any public relations campaign, the right message is required for the right audience. In face-to-face communication special care must be taken in selecting the target. The most useful targets are elite groups, opinion formers who tend to form the attitudes of the rest of the larger audience. Such persons must be sought out. They may be political leaders, teachers, religious figures, or perhaps even small shopkeepers. The key communicators are those persons upon whom others rely for their information and whose judgment is respected. Sociological research studies may be available to assist in identifying such individuals in a particular area. However, it is likely the police will have to rely on observation and their own judgment to determine the influential persons within a given society.

Time and Location for the Message

Efforts to disseminate information by face-to-face communication are dependent upon correct location and time. If a speech is to be made, it should be at a time when most of the potential target can attend and in a centrally located place. Individual contacts should be made when the situation is most apropos for conversation. It is necessary to select the time and location for the propaganda appeal when the target audience, either individually or collectively, is most psychologically receptive.

Just as verbal communications between men occur in many variations, so can public relations face-to-face communication be conducted with a variety of techniques. Among these techniques are the use of rallies, small status groups, group movements, social activities and direct "person-to-person" contact. In some cases the face-to-face communication network, as for example the small status group, may already exist. The officer then concentrates upon getting the group to receive and accept his message. In many instances, however, the officer must create a situation conducive to face-to-face communication, for example by organizing a meeting.

Large groups gathered together to be informed and entertained are susceptible to manipulation and may be stimulated to support a particular cause. Crowds or groups are usually drawn together by a common interest and may enjoy a feeling of participation or belonging subject to a continual flow of mutual stimulation. Under such conditions public relations messages can find acceptance among substantial numbers drawn from different socioeconomic levels. Meetings—if they are effectively organized, the subject is interesting or vital and the speaker's personality is magnetic—can emotionally involve the audience in the police program.

Methods of organizing meetings depend upon the social groups involved and the subject matter of the meeting. Of major concern, too, are the time and location, staging, type of entertainment (dancing, singing, motion pictures, etc.), and timing for public relations appeal. The foregoing points up the need for considerable knowledge of the audience in order to conduct and organize a rally.

Small and tightly organized groups can be effectively employed to spread public relations appeals. By organizing such groups or using existing ones, the officer is able to extend his appeal to a selected target. Such status groups can be composed of the key communicators within the local community.

Group movements such as youth groups, religious organizations, and women's clubs, provide an opportunity for face-to-face communication for psychological operations purposes. Stimulation of group activity and community action toward a real or psychological goal which is in agreement with the aims of police public relations operations can help the police reach their objectives. Group movements themselves can expand the psychological impact of the propagandist's message by becoming the disseminators of propaganda.

Group cohesiveness can be stimulated through social activities. Activities appropriate to local customs—fiestas, festivals, picnics, dances, quasi-religious rites—serve to bring people together. Such gatherings may serve a public relations purpose in themselves besides offering an opportunity for face-to-face communication.

Advantages and Disadvantages

Face-to-face communication has, as does any other medium, advantages and disadvantages as an effective method for public relations. Among the advantages are audience selection, use in isolated areas, assessment of effectiveness and speed.

When mass media is employed, public relations messages will usually reach individuals for whom the message was not specifically intended. In face-to-face communication, however, the audience can be selected more deliberately with the appeal directed at the intended person or group. This, of course, can apply only during the initial contact as the message may be passed by word-of-mouth to others among an unintended audience.

In some areas mass communication media is ineffective because of a lack of television and radios, high illiteracy and inaccessability to the audience. In such areas the only method of communication may be by word-of-mouth. Public relations appeals through face-to-face communication become essential here, if there is to be real contact with the target audience.

An important aspect of the face-to-face situation is that the communicator is not only able to tailor his appelas to the target, but that he can judge by direct observation and response the effect of his propaganda appeals. If communication is not being achieved, the message can be modified on the spot. This factor alone emphasizes the potential effectiveness of the face-to-face situation.

In some instances face-to-face communication may be the most rapid method of dissemination of propaganda. Information can spread rapidly by word-of-mouth if conditions are correct. Thus, while face-to-face communication cannot be judged in terms of "fast" or "slow," at certain times face-to-face situations offer a swift means for public relations dissemination.

Face-to-face communication is a powerful tool which, if used correctly, can bring rich rewards. Controlled face-to-face communication is deliberate and requires planning just as with any other media. It must not be used only when necessary, but whenever possible.

LIAISON

Since the law enforcement agency is the servant of all the people, an advance accounting of proper stewardship will build the necessary community goodwill and confidence which is so necessary in time of crisis. If the people can be brought to realize that the law enforcement officials are doing the best job humanly possible in the day-to-day performance of their responsibilities, then the presumption of right action and proper conduct will be foremost in the minds of the citizenry when adverse criticism arises. Establishing good rapport with organizations in the community is not a one-shot affair. It cannot be done by a press release, literature, letters or phone calls. It requires across-the-table conversation on a continuing basis by competent staff personnel.

In a word, the police must establish liaison with the community. By liaison we mean as a "bond or connecting link, a coordination of activities, intercommunication between units acting as neighbors."

Methods of Establishing Liaison

The police cannot wait for the public to come to them, rather, they must aggressively seek out and make the acquaintance of individuals and associations, and must deliberately seek to arouse, promote and maintain an active concern for the public welfare within community organizations. To this end they should avail themselves of any and all opportunities to make face-to-face contacts and to speak to or assist various groups and clubs.

The police must inform the public fully, by all the means available, of the position of the police and give to the public information on police and their work, and promote frequent conferences with community organizations to discuss laws, policies and procedures of mutual interest. They must learn the conditions in the community, ascertain the reactions of the public to police problems, techniques and policies, supply knowledgeable speakers on the police and their work to various clubs, conduct public programs to show the caliber and preparedness of the police and demonstrate the effectiveness of police protection. The police must also establish an open-door policy by making it clear that the avenue is always open to anyone who wishes to visit the police facilities or to discuss problems and notify the police of the existence of problems. Finally, the police must solicit and evaluate advice, especially on matters pertaining to complex community problems, and assist community organizations in an advisory capacity.

Membership in community organizations by individual policemen should be encouraged. These members can assist in the association and identification of police with the local population. They also provide the police agency with excellent sources of information valuable to police and community planning.

OPEN DEPARTMENT

The first step is to take the shroud of secrecy off the police department, its operations and practices. Law enforcement is not an island within the community, remote and self-sufficient. It is a very important part of a complex society; police are the agents of this society. The public must be made aware of its involvement and its responsibilities. In many cases, public opinion is shaped adversely to the police department's interests through misinformation or even a complete lack of knowledge about a particular issue. Unfortunately, people are prone to fill in a void of information with conclusions, often "jumped-to," based on rumors and half truths which they may hear. When they are personally acquainted with a police official who has made a favorable impression upon them, this is much less likely to happen. Additionally, if the lines of communication are open and available, responsible members of the community will not hesitate to discuss matters with the police; they will have a ready source of information from which facts may be obtained.

SPEAKERS

Speakers from the police department should be made available to community groups to acquaint the members with the services provided them. These talks present the law enforcement officials with the opportunity to get their viewpoint across and increase the exposure of the police to the general community. The topic or subject area of the speech may be dictated by local problems or interests or the interest of the group itself. There are several points to keep in mind when approaching these groups. First, of course, it is to make known that the police department is available to perform this service and prepare several suggested areas of concern which might be subject for discussion. This requires that top speakers be selected and trained. A public contact bureau should be formed. Channels for assignment of speakers and approval of speeches must be established.

By forming a group of selected officers using approved material the best image can be projected. A prohibition against speeches without approval should be known and adhered to. In selecting the speaker, the department must have these questions in mind: Can he cope with a group? Can he answer questions not related to his speech? Can he think on his feet?

Within the framework of your city organization, the police department and the community, let it be known that requests are welcomed and are channeled in from any source to a designated official within your organization. Your representative should also solicit opportunities to have the police address various groups. Letters should be sent to desired groups of civic clubs and community organizations offering such service. Care should be exercised to insure that the group hears topics which bear on the community understanding.

It is important to remember to emphasize the affirmative aspects of police work rather than to condemn some group or organization or just to decry the lawlessness in the streets. It should be noted that these speeches are opportunities to get the people on your side, and this can be done most effectively if they have some positive points to grasp. There are many areas of law enforcement with which the public is acquainted. These positive, constructive aspects of police work should be emphasized. Records of groups, speeches and lectures should be kept by the responsible authority. A film library that can be used to educate the public should be started with a budgeted amount to be spent. Similar records on the films' use should be kept.

Some departments have found that the use of police training films serve as good mediums for describing the function of police in certain respects. These films not only indicate the type of training which an officer receives, but also get across the message regarding the role of the police department with respect to a particular problem.

Offers to Help

Whatever the form or subject, these contacts can be fruitful and rewarding to the police department. Often as a result of these contacts, the service group or organization will ask what they can do as individuals and as a group to assist the department in its task. The question of what they can do as individuals can be answered without much difficulty. The question of what these groups can do as an entity can be answered only with thought and preparation. It is important to reply quickly to these offers of help, so that the current enthusiasm of the group can be captured. Hopefully, several plans could be conceived prior to the need, so that the action of the department can be quick and decisive. The type of work which these groups can be called upon to do is varied. They might be willing financially to underwrite the publication of a safety pamphlet for the use of school children, sponsor an open house at the police department, buy some special materials or equipment which would aid the police department in the presentation of talks to other groups, or sponsor a television program on a certain aspect of police concern. The type of program which the police department would develop for the community cannot be specified here, but the need to think ahead and plan for such citizen assistance is critical if the department is going to use every opportunity presented to improve relations with the entire community.

LIAISON WITH CIVIL, FRATERNAL, PROFESSIONAL AND RELIGIOUS GROUPS

Introduction

In every area there are groups of citizens who have banded together into organizations and clubs designed to work toward some interest common to the various members. These groups are normally composed of parents, residents of the community, businessmen and professional men—people who have an inherent interest in the character, welfare and prosperity of the community. In addition, these organizations and individuals represent a general cross section of the community. The study of community activities reveals that they are often basically organized in accordance with racial, economic, occupational, religious, or social similarities and beliefs. Each community organization serves as a clearing house for information relevant to its activities and field of interest. Through them the police have the means to convey information to many in the community.

Police officials, through the sound relations achieved in the civic action program, can enlist the support of civic organizations. By favorably influencing their members, maintaining open support of police impartiality and demanding peaceful settlement, these organizations can assist in the suppression of mob action.

Each command should maintain a file of such organizations located within its jurisdiction. Officers' membership in civic and business clubs should be encouraged. With active participation in programs in the area, the police show police willingness to be of service. City fathers should contribute the funds for such membership. Many cities now pay for membership in police fraternal and alumni groups. Why should they not sponsor police membership in the civic groups that are a part and parcel of our community life?

It should be stressed that the police must avoid aligning themselves with one civic group or service club to the exclusion of others. Membership in individual service clubs should be undertaken only with an understanding of limited participation. The police should avoid election as an officer or serving on committees where their influence might be used to the advantage of the club, or where such advantage might be apparent. Their position in the community might be jeopardized by such alignment. The police may mobilize the interest of clubs in constructive action on minority problems and give it direction by pointing out specific things these agencies could do to ease various problems of minority groups and to promote harmonious relations.

The National Exchange Club is an outstanding example of what a civic organization can do nationally and locally to promote law enforcement. Each year it sponsors National Crime Prevention Week. It supplies kits which contain suggestions for news releases, editorials, radio and television shows. One of the important sections of the kit is that devoted to educational material which can be reproduced and distributed to the citizens of the community warning them of dangers and the simple steps they can take to protect themselves and their property. In addition, there is excellent material directed to parents and children to aid in the battle against juvenile delinquency.

The Kiwanis International has also taken an active role in aiding law enforcement through public relation and educational activities. The police should recognize, assist and appreciate these efforts.

Many communities have focused citizen attention on local police and the job which the police do for the people by means of a law enforcement week. In some cases local businessmen's organizations sponsor a police appreciation week. During such a week, the police are generally the subjects of an intensive publicity campaign in their support. Speeches are given to all segments of the community, and ceremonies are often held in honor of the police. Often during these weeks, special activities are held which focus the community's interest on the police. Service clubs in cooperation with the departments, or the departments themselves, hold community-wide open houses of police facilities. Special demonstrations are given in new police techniques. Of course, these open houses need not be held only in conjunction with a law enforcement week. They may be held at any appropriate time. Special tours of police facilities can be arranged by appointment throughout the year for interested groups or individuals. In such a situation, the police have an opportunity to inform the citizens of the positive as well as the punitive aspects of law enforcement. Such tours remove some of the mystical qualities which confornt citizens in their contact with the police.

Besides open houses by the police department during a law enforcement week or at other appropriate times, some departments emphasize the importance of citizen participation in law enforcement by presenting special awards to those citizens who have made particular contributions to law enforcement work during the year. This is the reverse of programs sponsored by many service clubs of presenting awards to the police officers who have made particular contributions to the community during the previous year. Both of these programs offer good opportunities to publicize the nature of the relationship between individual citizens and individual police officers.

Religious Leaders

Religious leaders in the community can be of much assistance to the police. They should be the moral leaders of the community and the conscience of society. They have a most vital interest and must play a commanding role in maintaining law and order.

The police must get to know the community's religious leaders. Both must recognize that their ends are identical and that they can and must help each other. Each must learn the problems of the other. One way to bring the problem of law enforcement home is to have the clergy spend time observing the police in action, not only at police headquarters but in the field by riding in police cars or night patrol.

It is suggested that the police and clergy of all faiths conduct a series of meetings to inquire into problems. A joint steering committee can be organized to continually study changing community problems and what the police and clergy can do working together to provide a better community.

PUBLIC PERSONALITIES

Some departments have found that it is valuable to work with public figures who act as public relations men for the police. Sports figures or television personalities can give added luster and increase public attention to a police public relations campaign. However, caution must be used in employing such figures to assist the police in their campaign to win community support. The role which these people play must be carefully thought out before they are sent into the field. Because a person is, for example, a great baseball player, does not necessarily make him an expert on the police in a particular community. Furthermore, the people realize this. If such a person went out into the community and started saying that the police are great guys in this community and we ought to help them because of this, the average citizen might well think, "What does he know?" If, on the other hand, this personality's message was that he has found that cooperation with the police has been valuable to him in many ways in his own particular career, many people would take notice and listen. Thus, although these celebrities can be valuable aides in a public relations campaign, their role must be carefully analyzed so that there is not an adverse reaction in the community as a whole.

PRIVATE SECURITY

One profession that deserves special mention is private security. The men who are in this field are closely allied with the police in training, experience, work and goals. Both groups have everything to gain by cooperating and by maintaining close liaison.

Unfortunately this has not always been the case. Often, business management expects local police to provide protective services which are impossible for a police department to deliver. Even the best police departments cannot provide the constant surveillance required to protect major industries and business establishments adequately. Big business must protect itself by providing capable and responsible security officers.

It is law enforcement's job to sell business management on its obligation to provide its share of its own protection. A suggestion that management make some provision for its own protection should not be interpreted as an unwillingness on the part of law enforcement to provide a tax-bought service, nor should overtures by business to provide their own internal security be viewed as a vote of "no confidence" in the local police department.

There should be somewhere where the police department can say to industry that the necessary-protection problems are beyond the scope of the local police department and that industry, itself, must take certain steps in providing security personnel. The criteria for this would be repeated losses through burglaries, substantial employee stealing and chronic vandalism. At times, routine police patrol may not be sufficiently effective in these areas. A police department can evaluate industrial crime patterns. If self-help protective devices appear to be inadequate, there should be no hesitancy on the part of an informed law enforcement agency to make recommendations to these industries to employ full-time plant protection.

It is therefore well to stop for a moment and consider how one can complement the other.

A good plant security officer aids police in numerous ways; for instance, crime prevention and investigation are the major concern of industrial security. The establishment of a fire protection system and the training of employee fire brigades is certainly another vital part of the plant-protection work load.

Of course, the assistance rendered to the local police in the removal, with a minimum amount of notoriety, of employees wanted for crimes falls into the lap of industrial security. The control of pedestrian and vehicular traffic in and around the property of the industry is also important. Enforcement of health, sanitation, and safety rules, while not police related, may have a remote connection to the ultimate preservation of peace.

Industrial security's responsibility of establishing and maintaining an adequate system of locks and keys is an outstanding example of crime prevention at work. The system for employee and visitor identification, which is usually developed and controlled by industrial security, is another act of crime prevention. Of course, the patrolling of buildings and premises and the inspection of special hazards and fences on a continuing basis affect the ultimate security of the plant and the community. Even an unarmed guard is a deterrant to some types of crime by his mere presence on the premises.

Law enforcement has a responsibility to constantly advise and assist private security in the performance of its job. To accomplish this, it is good public relations to review from time to time with the industrial community methods and ways they can help.

Again, law enforcement and industrial security should develop a check list of needs and contributions which dovetail into each other. Crime prevention techniques in the hands of the professional police can provide a great deal of assistance to plant security. The police can, for instance, patrol areas where employees park and develop programs to prevent stealing from autos.

The physical facilities and equipment of the department, the labs and special investigative equipment and so forth, should be made available to industrial security units. Many departments permit industrial security personnel to take police training in the regular police academy. This, of course, is probably the surest way of insuring a good liaison between security people and local police. It also builds mutual confidence.

When department policy permits, records and arrest registers should be offered without hesitation. They are invaluable to plant security people. Labor disputes, fraud cases and shoplifting are all incidents which require close work between industrial security and local police. Police specialists, particularly in the case of shoplifters, can be of great assistance to store-security people by pointing out and identifying known thieves.

LIAISON WITH GOVERNMENT ORGANIZATIONS

Liaison with Legal Department

It is important to make use of the city attorney and the district attorney. We must bear in mind that our democratic form of government holds the legislatures responsible for enactment of laws, the courts and legal departments for interpretation of these laws, and the police for enforcement of these laws. It is suggested that the police agency take the initiative in requesting the local legal representative to do the following:

1. Research federal, state and local laws pertaining to the control of demonstrations, riots, crowds and gatherings, and the many other situations which may develop; and further, that he study and know the effects of court interpretations of the various laws and ordinances.

2. That he teach this subject to members of the police department, thus giving the men on the beat and the officer on the street a thorough and practical knowledge of the legal aspects of this problem. More detailed and thorough instructions should be given to supervisory personnel on the same subject matter.

3. Assist in advising minority groups regarding the legal responsibility of the law enforcement agency in the handling of these matters.

4. Be present for immediate and on-the-spot opinions in instances which could occur or have resulted in violence.

For many years we have discussed the problem of law enforcement officers being called upon to make legal decisions without legal advice. Frequently it took months and years of legal action by the courts before deciding whether or not we had acted wisely. When demonstrations or other incidents are scheduled and notice is received in advance, it is considered advisable to arrange for a legal advisor to be available on the spot.

There is need also for more adequate communication of court decisions to the police. In some small departments important decisions may never become known to the individual police officer. Even in large departments there are serious problems. The greatest impact upon police practice may come from the day-to-day decisions of the trial courts. Usually these are not written and are, as a consequence, passed on by word of mouth from the officer involved in the case to other officers in the department. In the process, a great deal of distortion inevitably occurs. Even when appellate opinions are available, it is evident that they are not written in a way that makes it easy for police to understand what they are expected to do.

Liaison with City and County Officials and Agency Officials

It is entirely possible that city and county officials, including elected officials, may give cause for concern and be a greater problem at times than some of the demonstrators. An extremely publicity-conscious official, lacking an understanding of the problem and a realization of its seriousness, may make public statements which tend to destroy previous police planning. Therefore, it is important that the police inform their city and county officials of the seriousness of a situation, keep them fully advised of its progress and solicit their cooperation. Only in this way can one hope to convince them not to make irresponsible or inflammatory statements to the press and public, nor make rash promises or threats which cannot and should not be fulfilled.

Agencies

Certain local public agencies which can supply the police department with valuable information are the housing, welfare, health, fire and building departments. In many instances the police can point out needs which these other agencies can meet or help solve. The records of such agencies often contain information that would help the police develop their preventive program. Moreover, the inspectors and other employees of these agencies will often discover facts concerning possible tension areas and danger points that would be a valuable supplement to police intelligence work in this field.

It is axiomatic that the general welfare of any segment of the public contributes to or detracts from its voluntary compliance of the forces of law and order. The needs of specific members of society which come to police attention and which can be corrected by other agencies should be reported as a matter of routine procedure. The police can aid the individual further by pointing out to him the facilities and services which are available and arranging for the person in need to secure these services.

Cooperation with other city departments and public agencies can perhaps be most easily and advantageously initiated. The police in many areas are already actively cooperating with school authorities in handling problems created by interracial strife among school children.

Liaison with Other Law Enforcement Officials
and Military Commanders

Police should cultivate an acquaintance and rapport with other law enforcement officials of surrounding communities and members of state and federal law enforcement, regulatory agencies and military units. Police should participate in area police officials' organizations, where they exist. A cooperative attitude with these officials will generally produce favorable results later when problems of mutual interest arise.

Definite arrangements should be made, before there is any sign of trouble on the horizon, regarding procedures by which the assistance of other law enforcement agencies can be obtained in the shortest possible time if there should be a serious disturbance in the area. As the procedure for obtaining such help varies, it is essential to know exactly what steps must be taken to obtain assistance from each of the available forces, to have detailed plans worked out with the heads of such forces and, if possible, to have all necessary papers drawn up ahead of time, requiring only signatures and dating to make them effective.

ADVISORY COMMITTEES

The police should actively seek the cooperation of a bar association-police committee. The lawyer who represents a defendant may be the very person to open the door to understanding, cooperation and the formation of such a committee. Through such committees both organizations become enlightened and views are exchanged.

Let us consider being a part of nonpolice government problems. If a police-lawyer committee could work, would not a similar police-chamber of commerce committee function well on civic affairs, gatherings, parades; or a merchant-police group resolving parking problems; or a police-business bureau function well on bad checks and fraud; or a police-community-complaints-neighborhood committee operating on the communities' complaints?

The main point is that these committees report back and, based on these recommendations, the department formulates policy that informs and directs others. Indeed, it might be well to go even further and consider arbitration committees.

The customary role of the police in waiting until an eruption has occurred before participating must be discontinued. Our role as impartial aides to mediation must be enlarged. The practice of participating in community ventures toward peaceful solutions of community problems must be enhanced to avoid our subsequent participation with physical, forceful suppression.

ARBITRATION COMMITTEES

Police officials might well promote the formation of a special arbitration committee that will seek the settlement of the problem that created the disorder. The arbitration committee, since it represents both viewpoints of the disturbance, can be effectively employed as a supervisory panel to oversee the restoration and maintenance of law and order. Arbitration committees may effectively assist in the following important areas:

1. The coordinating of remedial efforts of participating public and semi-public agencies.
2. The protecting of the community officials from the influences of selfish minority groups that might act contrary to the public's interest.
3. The influencing of public officials to act in the interests of public welfare by supporting the adoption of desirable programs and the discontinuance of those considered to be undesirable.
4. Seeking public support of programs designed in the public interest.
5. Winning public cooperation in the form of compliance with regulations and active intolerance of their violations.

COMMUNITY ACTIVITIES

Another area of a public relations program is police department participation in community activities. Of course, this aspect of a police-community relations program is separate and apart from the individual efforts of police officers in behalf of the community, which are undertaken by them as private citizens. Their contribution to the image of the department can be real and meaningful, and such individual contributions should be encouraged by the department, but they do not fill the gap for organized participation by the department in the projects of the community. Department participation provides another positive aspect to the dimensions of police work which can be translated by the citizens into beneficial relations with the police, i.e., greater respect for the department and the individuals therein.

Police participation on the departmental level in community activities might be classified as nonessential, nonpolice functions and therefore not to be undertaken by a department. However, as an increasing emphasis is placed on crime prevention—which it must be—the departmental participation takes on important aspects of police work. This is but another integral phase of the job of selling the police. Depending on the particular activity, the departmental participation can attack the cause and/or the effect of poor police relations with the community as a whole. Assuming that, in part, the cause of poor community relations is often the by-product of poverty and ghetto living, participation in community affairs can help to alleviate these conditions, and therefore positively affect these relationships. Furthermore, these conditions set up barriers in communications which manifest themselves in poor relations between citizens and the police. Participation in community activities can give beneficial exposure to the department and its motives of protection of and service to the public. For example, the lack of recreation may cause problems and tension. The police might undertake a program to improve recreation facilities. Thus the department would be getting at the underlying cause and also, at the same time, improving the communication which had deteriorated because of the underlying cause. Thus, participation in community activities can give a twofold benefit to the participating department.

Types of Activities

The types of activities which might be undertaken by the department on a community-wide scale can be classified into two general areas: first, those projects which are directly related to the department or its activities; and second, those activities which are for the betterment of the community as a whole and only provide indirect and collateral benefits for the department.

The types of community activities undertaken by the department which would be directly related to departmental activities can be many and varied and would run the whole gamut of police functions. The particular program adopted or undertaken in any one area would depend on the unique needs of that community. Nevertheless, certain program areas which have been successfully attempted can be generalized and categorically stated to provide guidelines in this area.

One type of activity or program which is widely used by many departments is the campaign to eliminate or decrease certain crimes. Merchants are instructed on ways to prevent the bad- or forged-check passer from succeeding. Citizens in general are instructed on ways to prevent, or what to do in case of, a robbery or burglary. Women are cautioned on ways to prevent sexual attacks. These are but a few of the many and varied programs which the police can conduct for the benefit of the community. These programs should be emphasized as being a service to the public. The program can be conducted through the aid of the mass media and pamphlets for distribution to the public. The topics of the campaign can be the subject of speeches to local groups.

The resources of the police departments have often been called into play during the Christmas season for the benefit of underprivileged citizens of the community. The departments in cooperation with other civic organizations have sponsored food collection, toy repair and collection, and clothes collection for the unfortunate at Christmas.

With precincts in most areas, the police are able to act as central collection agencies throughout the city in such projects. Many departments have undertaken such projects in recent years and have been rewarded by the goodwill of the community and, in particular, those low income families whom they assisted.

Police departments have cosponsored with neighborhood associations "clean-up days." As a result of this type of program, it is possible that the residents will have greater pride in their neighborhood and greater self-confidence. Such an attitude should help in their relationship with the police. Also, it is beneficial to have these residents have the experience of working with the police while the police are trying to help them help themselves. Again the idea is brought across that the police department wants to help them and is willing to cooperate with them.

Another aspect of these activities in which the police engage for the benefit of the community is the creation of demonstration units within the department which appear at civic events as police representatives. These units would include police bands, drill teams, motorcycle drill teams and pistol teams, among others. Such units can promote the image of police efficiency and give added color to, or stimulate interest in the activities of the department, as well as providing some recreation for the officers themselves. Not only are these units something of which the citizens can be proud and in which they are interested, but they are satisfying for the department as well.

COMMUNITY AID OFFICER

Another function that will enhance the prestige of law enforcement is a community aid officer. To the public, the police represent the answer to all of today's problems. If a family is without food, the police are called. An employee is detained in court all day as a witness and the employer calls the police. School buses delay motorists getting to work, and again it is assumed this is a police problem. Although the police are often unable to offer service in these situations, they should do everything possible to see that the individual in need is referred to the person, organization or agency that can help.

Whenever possible do all you can to satisfy the needs of the public, and remember that these needs are psychological as well as physical. Stop grievances and frustrations before they accumulate. If it seems wise and expedient and if it is possible, do not hesitate to adjust rules and regulations or to shift emphasis in order to justify new demands. However, do not, of course, compromise your own interests or goals in the process.

MASS MEDIA

Naturally when considering a public relations program, one of the first areas of concern is the effective use of the mass media such as newspapers, television and radio. The nature of police relationship with the press is primarily one which is concerned with the internal organization of the department and the attitude of the press. A positive program of public relations is a matter requiring separate organization and planning. The emphasis here is the type of public relations program that can be presented in this manner.

The most usual type of public relations program conducted through the news media is that which publicizes the special activities of the department. These might be programs conducted in conjunction with a law week or police week or tours of police functions. The public media might also be used to publicize special services of the department which would contribute to the image of the department as a community service agency, such as special vacation patrols for citizens whose homes are left unoccupied or special campaigns such as the prevention or reduction of the number of stolen automobiles. These traditional uses of news media must not be forgotten when any campaign is mounted, but it should also be recognized that the news media can be used for other public relations functions.

The medium of television can present many opportunities to communicate with the public in meaningful and resourceful methods. Short spots can be used to publicize police-sponsored events. Debates and inquiries, perhaps of only five to eight minutes of duration in conjunction with a local news program, can be held in which items of interest or public concern can be discussed. With such an approach, all of the benefits of this medium can be capitalized upon for the gain of the police department. Similar programs can be initiated on the radio. With the cooperation of those stations which gear their programming to teen-agers, special programs and messages can be conceived which would be directed at that group.

The press can also be used in imaginative ways to improve police-community relations. A "Know Your Officer" column in the local newspaper permits the public to associate a name with a face, or at least see a familiar face in a police uniform, as well as permitting the officer's viewpoint and background to be described. A weekly or monthly column in which current police programs, problems or attitudes are discussed is of value. Under such columns the police can articulate their positions and also can emphasize positive police programs, which the citizens might not understand, for the betterment of the community. These columns might be placed in the general press of the community or in the press which directs itself toward a particular segment of the population. These columns or articles might also be released to those organizations which have their own local publications such as the labor unions or service clubs. To achieve publication in either the special group press or the minority press, close cooperation between the police and the publishers would, of course, be necessary. In considering the minority press, the foreign language press of the community should not be ignored as sources of publicity, even though such contact might require special work.

SLOGANS

Over the years, many agencies have produced a popular accepted slogan, idea, or concept which caught on in the public imagination. One of the earliest and certainly most popular was the FBI "Ten Most Wanted" list.

Riverside County in California has used and proved the effectiveness of educational slogans in news releases broadcast over local radio stations and feature stories published in area newspapers. The sheriff's office of that county has made the effort to develop phrases which would have an appeal to the audience. Some phrases were most appropriate when heard in a broadcast or speech, others when read. All phrases stressed the importance of professional law enforcement in terms of the individual, his family and his community.

A further test imposed was that each phrase must present law enforcement as an established authority. As much as possible, an effort was made to remind each citizen of his responsibility to the success of his community law enforcement program. Every effort was made to avoid an inference that law enforcement was not capable of accomplishing its job and was attempting to plead or cajole the public to come to the rescue.

The following is a list of those slogans which proved most effective:

1. The badge of the police is your badge of protection. It represents their authority to enforce your laws. Obey them . . . and insist that others do too!
2. The safety of your family depends a great deal upon law enforcement. The effectiveness of law enforcement depends a

great deal upon you. Obey the law . . . support strict law enforcement!

3. Respect the authority of the law by obeying the law.
4. Dishonoring the law is a step backwards. Keep in step with your community. Obey the law . . . support strict law enforcement!
5. Keep the peace . . . always obey the law!
6. The law is your protection—obey it and protect others!
7. Others are obeying the law for your protection. Obey the law and protect others!
8. Protect others—obey the law!
9. Don't be outside the law. Learn the inside facts—law enforcement is everybody's business!
10. Don't "lay down the law"—uphold it!
11. Reward your family with the protection they deserve—support strict law enforcement!
12. Only you can prevent crime—obey the law and see that others do too!
13. Crime doesn't pay—but strict law enforcement does!
14. You are the most important member of the law enforcement team. You call the signals—we hold the line!
15. Don't gamble on your future. Play it safe—obey all laws!
16. Pledge your support for strict law enforcement—vote for law and order!
17. Law observance is everybody's business!
18. Law enforcement means law and order!
19. Respect the need for "law and order." Respect the need for strict law enforcement!
20. Understanding—and obeying the law is everybody's business!
21. Respect the law of the land—support strict law enforcement!
22. Our country is founded upon law and order. Respect your country—respect your laws—help law enforceemnt keep law and order!
23. Law enforcement's job is the protection of life and property—your life and your property—help law enforcement by obeying the law!
24. Think "law and order." Obey the law—respect its authority!
25. You have given law enforcement the job of enforcing your laws. Respect these laws—respect this authority!
26. Cooperation is the key to law and order. Use this key wisely by obeying the law—and by respecting its authority!
27. An informed society recognizes its responsibilities—and the responsibilities of their police who enforce the law!
28. The strength of a country lies in the strength of its citizens—

respect and obey the law of the land!

29. Obey the law—respect strict law enforcement!
30. The badge of law enforcement is your shield of protection. Honor the badge by obeying the law—strengthen the shield by respecting its authority!
31. Effective law enforcement depends upon effective cooperation. Knowing the law—and obeying it—is everybody's business!
32. Give your childern the opportunity to enjoy the protection of the law—set a good example—support strict law enforcement!
33. Shoulder the responsibilities of your community by letting law breakers know that you support strict law enforcement!
34. Law enforcement officers are fighting a war—your war against the criminal. You cannot afford to sit on the sidelines!
35. No one has the right to do wrong—everyone has the duty to insist upon law and order!
36. Law enforcement is everybody's business!
37. Shoulder the responsibilities of your community. Stand for law and order—support strict law enforcement!
38. Law enforcement's job is to keep your community safe for you and your family. It's your job too. Make law enforcement everybody's business!
39. The law of the land is the last word—the first word is to obey this law!
40. Always obey the law. You are not safe without it.
41. The law protects you—obey it and protect others!
42. The People of the State *vs.* Crime . . . How do you plead?

Chapter II

YOUTH ACTIVITIES

INTRODUCTION

Dᴜʀɪɴɢ ᴛʜᴇ ᴘᴀsᴛ twenty-five years, youths have grown up without the opportunity to know Officer "Clancy" as a friendly authority figure. It is clear that budget-conscious local governments have depersonalized the policeman for the economy and speed provided by mobility.

The alienation does not only involve youth in poor neighborhoods, for the most rapid increase in delinquency and lowered esteem for policemen is occurring in suburbia among middle-class youth. Hence, there is a need for a serious preventive program actively directed toward the adolescent group. Youngsters are numerous and active in every riot. The impressionability of youth makes them a danger point in any tension situation because they lack experience, which causes them to reject anything other than peaceful mediation of differences. They are sometimes the innocent tool of intolerant adults, but they can also be a moving force behind community violence.

More important, today's delinquent is tomorrow's adult. As he is molded now, he will be in the future. Thus it is doubly important to reach out and give him the direction he needs. The police can and must be active in this area.

PERSONAL CONTACT

Public attitudes are in part formed by the way children are handled and treated by police. Indeed children can do much to assist in the creation and maintenance of a favorable image. Police officials might appropriately consider ways and means of gaining the respect and admiration of the children.

Children of both minority and majority groups are usually

attracted to the police uniform. If the officer is friendly and helpful to them, if he occasionally stops to visit and exchange pleasantries with them, he can establish a grass-roots relationship which can be of great benefit. Indeed this unaffiliated informal conversation approach is outstandingly successful in establishing contacts and fostering understanding and respect.

LIAISON WITH SCHOOLS

A primary step in any youth program is the development of close cordial liaison with the schools and, more specifically, the school officials. These school officials can not only provide the permission for the police to carry on the program which they have organized, but also can provide suggestions for other programs which might provide more effective communication with the youth of the community.

The goals of the police and the educators are the same, for the building of respect for law is a central purpose of public education. The schools should shape every activity and every curriculum to build in the understanding, habits and commitments implied in law-abiding, loyal citizenship.

Our educators must instill, by their daily actions, a belief in our nation's system of laws and in our system of government. There are several ways to build respect for law, but the best approaches to meeting this challenge undoubtedly will be developed through the teachers' daily contacts with students, and the stressing of the basic principles of obedience to law, respect for others, mastery of self and joy in service.

Principals, deans of boys and girls, and athletic directors should be encouraged to undertake educational and preventive programs designed to minimize or prevent friction between children of different groups. School teachers, for example, can teach the children in their classes racial tolerance and common courtesy. They can make a further important contribution to harmonious racial relationships by explaining to their students proper methods of handling incidents involving members of different races. Fights that begin among school children add to group tension and sometimes develop directly into fights between adults. Most schools and playgrounds could do more than they now do to combat such antagonism among children. Many of them would undertake educational and preventive programs if the police were constantly pointing out the needs and dangers in concrete terms.

It is highly desirable that the police develop close liaison with school and playground authorities in setting up programs calculated to prevent or minimize friction between children of different racial groups. For example, the junior police, school boys who guide traffic near schools before and after school hours, are trained by the police department. As part of this training the boys should be taught to discourage clashes or fights among their school companions, especially between members of different national or racial groups. When such fights occur in spite of the efforts of the junior police, the police department in cooperation with the public school officials should be used to straighten matters out and prevent grudges from developing. In such cases the parents of the quarreling individuals are often brought into the picture and the difficulties are worked out in their presence. This program tends to prevent children's quarrels from being taken up by their parents and also helps the children to develop good attitudes at an impressionable age, so that they are less likely to be troublemakers when they grow up.

The teacher is also in a position to learn from the children the general attitudes of the homes the children represent, for the attitudes of the children will generally reflect the feelings of the parents. This puts them in a position to make valuable suggestions concerning preventive police work.

Firm cooperation between them will do much to curb the activities at the close of school each day of undisciplined roving mobs or groups. Teachers should make it plain that misconduct during or after school will not be tolerated. The police department should follow up by providing close surveillance of student behavior as the students move from school to home.

Serious thought should be given to the proposal that the theory, necessity and actual elements of criminal and civil law be taught in both elementary and high school with an emphasis upon elementary school and criminal law. By-products of a school program in law could be a greater respect for law enforcement officers, making it less expensive and more satisfying for the police to carry out their mission, an increase in the recruiting base, and a comparable increase in police efficiency through a constant source of high caliber personnel. Psychiatrists and psychologists tell us that attitudes and prejudices are, for the most part, formed sometime between ages five and twelve, and the next most impressionable period is during the teens. If this premise is true, the greater portion of the education program should be concentrated in these age groups.

The material to be covered could include the following:

1. An appreciation of the necessity of laws and regulations in governing our democracy.
2. Freedoms guaranteed under the law.
3. Pranks versus crimes.
4. Auto theft.
5. Disorderly conduct.
6. Petty larceny.
7. Use of weapons.
8. Shoplifting.
9. Unlawful assembly.
10. Truancy and vandalism.
11. Use of liquor and narcotics.
12. The criminal and juvenile courts.
13. The consequences of a criminal record.

Educators can aid the police in still another way. Colleges and universities have a great wealth of practical knowledge that can and should be imparted to the police service. In or near each community there are institutions of higher learning. One significant role which these institutions can play is teaching the behavioral sciences in police training programs.

The police, themselves, can take an active part in the school program in many ways which bring the police into direct personal contact with the students. At schools, especially at the lower grade levels, the police have an organized audience which encompasses the entire spectrum of society. At the higher grade levels the audience is thinned out by dropouts, but still the majority of the youth can be reached.

True, the limited contact which the police have with the juveniles at school cannot have the effect that the environment which the child is subjected to every day has. However, such contacts can correct misconceptions and fortify correct attitudes toward the law enforcement officer.

The programs carried on in school generally encompass a threefold purpose. First, they educate the children as to their responsibility as citizens in the community. The policeman is uniquely qualified to aid the child in this respect, for he has a wealth of practical experience which enables him to bring this point home to the students.

Second, they contribute to the safety of the child and the prevention of crimes. Officers can teach the child about bicycle and pedestrian safety. At the high school age, the police can cooperate with the driver's education program. Programs can be presented by police on the dangers of narcotics or on practical suggestions about how to avoid the "friendly strangers." All of these areas are within the particular knowledge of the police, and programs in schools can put that knowledge to practical use.

Third, they teach the children to know the police officer as a friend and helper rather than a fear figure. At the same time the officer sees the children in a situation when the children are not breaking the law. Thus, by personal contact, the erroneous stereotypes that each group has of the other are destroyed and preexisting favorable impressions are strengthened.

Let us now consider more specific programs. In the lower grades an effort should be made to introduce the children to policemen and also to provide basic safety instruction. This is done by having police officers speak to the children. In conjunction with lectures on school safety, many departments pass out safety pamphlets, which may vary in form. Some use a comic-book-type format, others a picture story and still others a safety coloring book. Also along this pedestrian safety line, a department might set up a junior safety patrol. The students selected for this patrol are given instruction on helping students to cross the street at locations near the school and providing assistance to the police during school hours.

Another danger which police can lecture children on is the

problem of child molesting. The police can not only warn the children of the danger, but can also instruct the children on steps which they might use to help in the apprehension of child molesters. These lectures are particularly effective in marshaling parental support for the efforts of the police and can assist in improving the image of the police as protectors as well as the apprehenders.

The police may organize junior police and distribute badges to the students. In this way the students become associated with law enforcement and are made aware of their responsibilities as citizens. Demonstrations are also extremely effective with this young age group. The police can show the effectiveness of their dog teams in action, how the patrol cars operate, and how the police respond to calls for assistance.

Attempts to reach junior and senior high school students present difficult problems. Often these children are more sophisticated and cynical. They do not respond as readily to the traditional appeal to support law enforcement officers. Rather, means must be found to reach their special interests and mold the public relations process to their frame of reference.

Thus the lecture and study of law enforcement in the community is of limited effectiveness. A more fruitful field is that of automotive safety. It affords the police a great opportunity to communicate with most of the students. This communication can cover not only the traffic laws, but also what to do in case the students are stopped for a traffic violation. These lessons can be given in conjunction with the compulsory driver's education program and also with the auto shop which many of the boys take as a subject. Preventive driving can also be taught by a police officer. These contacts not only have a beneficial effect because of the safety lessons which are given, but also because the police have the opportunity to participate in discussion with the students when the police are not arresting them or involved in any other way because of a violation of the law.

In many cities police perform a public service of conducting baby-sitting classes for the girls of the community. The girls are trained in certain basic safety measures which they should know as well as procedures which should be followed when they take such a job. Employers of baby sitters are also provided with certain guidelines in this situation.

FAMILY

The family is the basis of our society, and it is here that the police program should begin, for if there is a strong cohesive family unit, there is less likelihood of delinquency. Thus the police should do everything in their power to strengthen the family. To do this the police should establish youth activities which foster greater parent interest and assist in the suppression of juvenile delinquency.

The police can also make contact with the parents through the schools. The parents can be reached indirectly through the pamphlets which the children receive when the police officers lecture to the children. They will be contacted personally at parent clubs and parent-teacher association meetings. Most all of the areas which are discussed with the students are subjects of concern for the parents also. Parents are concerned about the intricacies of traffic safety and protecting their child from child molesters. The efforts to communicate with the parents on steps to prevent any harm to their children and to keep their children from violating any law not only serves the purpose of preventive law, but also allows these parents to see the police in the role of the protector. These communications will give the parents more confidence in the police and their role in society. Furthermore, the parents become more involved with their responsibility as citizens to enforce and support the law.

One area in which the police and the parents can cooperate is the setting of standards for teen-age conduct in the community. This is an age-old problem in any community and for most parents. What is acceptable social conduct? When this conduct is set out with the cooperation of the students themselves, the parents and the police have something to fall back on when teen-age misconduct is present. These standards also have the advantage of allowing closer regulation, in a preventive sense, of teen-age activities. Parents are happy to receive basic instructions from the police on how to run a party so that it does not get out of hand. The police, with or without the direct cooperation of the parent organizations, may sponsor dances to keep the children occupied. Such recreation affords an outlet for their energy and desire to do something. Often they fill a needed gap in organized recreational activities in the community. Furthermore, these dances allow the police another chance to cooperate and communicate with the youth of the community. This spirit of cooperation can well carry over in other areas of police-juvenile relations.

Again, though these events might seem to be nonpolice functions, they do serve a preventive function in the aspect that the children are kept off the streets, and also in the aspect that there is greater communication between the two groups—certainly desirable police goals.

Another program which has been instituted by various departments in connection with parents groups at schools is the "block parent" or "block mother project." Although the purpose or form of the project may vary from community to community, the basic structure involves the selection of persons within a neighborhood who serve as a contact with law enforcement officials. The participating individuals are identified to the community in some cases by placards in the windows of their homes. In some cases the function of the block mother or parent is to be alert for suspicious persons loitering around the route to, or premises of, schools and other problems to which the attention of the police should be called. In other cases the function of the program is to designate persons who are available to assist juveniles who may need help, especially at times of emergencies. These programs have the advantage of involving citizens in police duties and of giving the police some needed assistance. This involvement of the citizen in the job of the protection of society is a hard goal to achieve, and this program goes a long way toward that end.

CITIZENSHIP PROGRAM

One method is to present a citizenship program designed to give to youth an understanding of why we have laws and how they help people. The program should be designed to attain the following goals:

1. To give parents and their children a better understanding of laws and the reasons why laws are necessary.
2. To develop closer family ties through joint participation of parent and child in the citizenship program.
3. To develop in the parents and their children an acceptance of what is expected of them in society today, both lawfully and morally.
4. To improve the image of the uniformed police officer by clarifying his role in our modern society and to give an understanding of his role in society.
5. To improve police-parent-child relations by working together in the proper atmosphere, induced by the program, which allows the learning of each other's problems.

The methods to be used would include classroom lecture, group discussion, question-and-answer periods, audio and audio-visual aids and demonstrations.

Homework assignments should be included in the program. They will be designed to promote family unity by having the children complete assignments under the guidance and instruction of their parents. The police officer assigned to patrol in their neighborhood discusses a current area-wide problem with the family in their home and solicits their help in abolishing the problem. Upon the children's return to class, these problems are discussed and solutions reached. Other homework assignments can require the reading of the newspaper, selecting a criminal offense, and reporting to the class the need for the particular law violated. The final homework assignment can be a paper written explaining why laws should be respected. Each assignment should be kept to approximately fifteen minutes with a minimum of effort on the part of the students, yet it can be very effectively used in classroom discussions. The paper "Why We Respect The Law" is also a method of testing to determine the amount of knowledge the class has gained.

As to the content of the program, it should first discuss

laws, how they are developed and the need for them. A group of laws, those most frequently violated, can be discussed by the class. Each participating family could be assigned a law to analyze, and then explain its need to the other members of the class.

Through lecture, demonstrations and discussion the class will learn that laws are made to help people. Learning that laws are safeguards built into our society for the protection of all people brings out the reason why we respect the law. Parents and children must be taught that an outward display of respect for the law commands the respect and acceptance in our society of anyone, regardless of economic or social level.

The development of law enforcement from the time of the "hue and cry" to the modern police department should be recounted. Parents and children should learn that an efficient, progressive police department can only exist where the people of a community have respect for law and an awareness of the police officers' role in our society.

Through lecture, group discussion and visual aids the class should learn the duties of a modern police officer and the functions of a police department. The need for law enforcement agencies must be explained by pointing out the various emergency services performed. The need for police officers becomes apparent to the class when the instructor relates to them the fact that police officers enforce laws made by the people, and that laws are for the protection of all people.

Rights and responsibilities of police is another important area to cover. Rights and responsibilities, for the purpose of the program, are defined as follows:

1. Right, the opportunity to do whatever we want as long as we do not violate the law.
2. Responsibility, is the duty of every citizen to respect the restrictions put on our rights by law.
3. Moral responsibility must also be covered in the program. This is defined as something people do that they know is right, even though there is no law requiring action on their part.

The parents and children learn that the right to enforce the law is given to the police by the people. Through experience and knowledge, people have learned that there must exist in our society an organization specifically designed to enforce the law, thus insuring the protection of the law for the decent people of a community.

The class will learn that police officers are responsible to the citizens of the community in which they serve. They are responsible for efficient, effective, unrelenting enforcement of the laws in their community. The parents and children must be taught that they, too, have the responsibility for law enforcement in their community. By acquainting the class with the problems encountered by police officers while discharging their sworn duties, the parents and children will learn that without public support law enforcement agencies are less effective in the prevention of crime in their community.

Finally, rights and responsibilities of parents and children should be covered. Particular emphasis should be placed on these as they affect the home, school and community. The laws explained in the previous sessions can be distributed to the members of the class. Family participation will be used, this time to determine the rights and the responsibilities that must go along with proper use of laws. It is explained that a law gives a person the right to do, or not to do, a particular act. If a person uses a law, he must also accept the inherent responsibility with which he is charged.

At the completion of the course, diplomas can be given to the attending children, and the families can be taken on a tour of the police facilities to show the modern and effective methods of police service with which the city is protected, and to impress upon them the fact that policemen are friendly and are necessary for our way of life.

TOURS OF POLICE DEPARTMENT AND COURTS

Tours of police facilities and the courts should be encouraged so that the students can see our legal system in operation. A more dramatic picture of police work can be given by allowing adults and students from both college and high school to actually spend time with police during their regular working hours. They might even be taken on regular night tours of the city in unmarked police cars in the company of experienced police officers. In this way youth will be directly involved in the depths of police work and see the police in action. This program will make present and future supporters for the police.

YOUTH ACTIVITIES

The police can energetically pursue a preventive campaign through the sponsorship of youth activities such as scout troops, youth camps and athletic leagues. Youth recreational programs are of such recognized value to public welfare that many police officers now work with such groups. Where youth recreation is inadequate, police can fulfill an important duty in preventing crime through youth recreational functions. These functions can eliminate conditions which may lead to youthful criminality. Police officers on an off-duty basis should volunteer as leaders or assistant leaders for youth groups. They would thus be in an excellent position to indoctrinate the children in the police philosophy and explain the offiical attitude of the department in interracial strife.

Several departments throughout the country have active police athletic leagues which work closely with playground authorities. Here the police can perhaps become most active in an educational program. The casual atmosphere fostered by mutual cooperation in recreational activities removes from the child's mind the punitive atmosphere too often associated with the police uniform and makes the child responsive to suggestions from the police. Under such a desirable atmosphere the undesirable attitudes of many children can be changed and a more tolerant attitude toward minority groups instilled. Police departments can sponsor an athlete-of-the-year award at local high schools. The police department can also take underprivileged children to major league sporting events or sponsor similar events for them.

Realizing that not all children are interested in athletics, other activities can also be sponsored by the police, such as bands, choirs, debating teams and art clubs. The police can sponsor speakers, clinics and safety programs for school and other youth organizations. The police appearing before youth groups is an excellent example of the approach which must be used.

TEEN-AGERS

Providing or participating in certain actiivties for the younger children of the city is a much easier task than reaching the teen-agers of the community. Teen-age cooperation and respect for the police or any authority is restricted. One of the more effective programs is police department sponsorship of car clubs. Under police control, these clubs may have organized drag racing or other such events. One important factor of such sponsorship is that the police can reach those teen-agers who otherwise would not be active in community affairs, children who would not be student leaders, kids who are probably most in need of nonpunitive contact with the police.

One of the comments that seems typical of teen-agers everywhere is that they have no place to go. The result is that they stand on street corners or spend the time driving around on the streets. The police in some communities have realized that such a situation contributes to their law enforcement burden and have sponsored or cooperated with teen centers in their community. Specialized contacts, an ongoing program with youth in a face-to-face relationship discussing problem areas, could serve to reduce youth hostility toward law enforcement and provide the mutual exchange of ideas between youth and law enforcement.

YOUTH COMMITTEES

Youth committees similar to district committees could be established to discuss problems unique to juveniles. These committees would also afford the juveniles an opportunity with an outlet to register their complaints and to make their thinking known.

Although the police must do all they can to eliminate the causes of delinquency, and thus delinquency itself, they are also bound to read the message in police records and employ protective tactics accordingly. This requires detailed knowledge of gang members, leaders and methods, as well as knowledge of their homes, their meeting places, their territories. It requires efficient juvenile enforcement.

JUVENILE ATTITUDE IMPROVEMENT PROGRAM

When an officer in the field has contact with a juvenile who, in the officers' opinion, has a poor attitude toward law enforcement, a memo should be forwarded to the juvenile division. The juvenile and his parent should be contacted at their home by a juvenile officer and an attempt made to discover reasons for, and solutions to, the hostile attitude. Again, as always, the stress is on prevention.

Chapter 12

POLICE-COMMUNITY RELATIONS COUNCILS

INTRODUCTION

To AID IN DEVELOPING community relations the police could organize police-community relations councils or committees in each district. These are voluntary, independent, self-constituted advisory bodies. They need not be established by ordinance and do not have to have legal sanction. They would not be, nor would they represent themselves as, an official or unofficial arm of the police department or any other official civic body or entity. Their sole interest is the promotion of better, closer and more effective relations between the police and the community for the welfare of the whole community.

The people who are members of the community relations committee must not have any special privileges under the law. These councils and committees should work under the leadership and direction of a special officer and staff designed to handle community relations. The police would be charged with the responsibility for coordinating their activities and supplying them the following assistance:

1. Mailing notices of meetings.
2. Planning special and suggested projects.
3. Acting as liaison with the commander and other officers in the district.
4. Duplicating the minutes of meetings.
5. Attending district and, if necessary, executive committee meetings.
6. Giving aid or assistance that may be needed or requested.
7. Publicizing activities by printing circulars, etc.
8. Contacting people that the committee cannot reach.

9. Inviting and mailing notices of meetings of the business-men.

10. Providing names, addresses and telephone numbers of commanders, juvenile officers, sanitation officers, school principals, teachers, etc.

GENERAL OBJECTIVES

The general objectives of the council and district committees are the following:

1. To plan and implement programs to acquaint individual citizens with their responsibilities in the maintenance and preservation of law and order.

2. To plan and carry out programs to acquaint the general public with the growing professionalization as well as the operations of the police force.

3. To support the continued professionalization of the police department.

4. To secure increased and greater public cooperation with the police by educating citizens in the preservation and maintenance of law and order.

5. To promote increased cooperation between the police and other community agencies.

6. To assist in crime prevention.

7. To develop neighborhood consciousness and neighborhood responsibility.

8. To work toward the reduction of the crime rate.

9. To support the highest police standards and the highest police efficiency.

10. To conduct a continuing survey of community needs which affect enforcement of law and the maintenance of peace in the community.

11. To publicize these needs as they are discovered and to transmit them to the duly authorized person or agency for appropriate action.

12. To serve and act as liaison between representatives of the police department and the neighborhood.

13. To consult regularly on common problems of law enforcement and public safety with the police department, district commander, district police personnel and the community.

14. To carry out, in cooperation with other existing organizations or agencies in the neighborhood, education programs designed to acquaint citizens in the neighborhood with the operation of their police department, and with individual citizens' responsibilities in the maintenance of law and order.

15. To maintain an information center through which the neighborhood problems can be promptly answered and referred to the proper person, organization or agency for resolution or clarification.

16. To serve as a base for neighborhood maintenance and improvement.

17. To refer to the police department all questions involving clarification of department policy.

18. To promote the utilization of existing facilities and agencies, such as scout troops, social centers, block organizations, welfare agencies and other community organizations.

19. To assist in preventing, reducing and eliminating racial and intergroup tensions, problems and conflicts.

20. To improve intergroup relations and communications between the police and the neighborhood.

21. To sharpen the awareness for the needs of public and/or private social agency services in the neighborhood.

Limitations

Problems and questions involving police policy must be referred to the police.

MEMBERSHIP

All adults residing or working in a district are eligible for membership in that district's police-community relations committee. Indeed it is desirable to have as broad a cross section of the district as possible, such as the businessmen who operate in the district, responsible residents who live in the district, professionals who work there, social workers, educators, clergymen, visiting nurses and recreation directors.

Most definitely, the leaders in their district, who are close to the "grass roots" and in an excellent position to influence the attitude of the ordinary citizen towards law enforcement, must be interested.

Above all, it must be nonpolitical, bipartisan and biracial. It must be so composed that it cannot be accused of being dominated by any single civic club, church, fraternal group or political organization. The committee must never be allowed to become an element of the political arena in any form, nor must it become a forum for causes of any type.

For a committee to be effective, active working members are essential. All members are expected to accept assignments to working subcommittees. All active members must agree to accept an assignment to act on at least one working subcommittee.

There can be two classes of membership. An active member is one who regularly attends the meetings of the district committee and is active in its functions. An associate member is any person who is interested in the goal of the district committee, wishes to receive all the information distributed by the committee, and is willing to cooperate with the committee; but who for any good reason cannot regularly attend the committee meetings and assume the role of an active member.

DUTIES OF MEMBERS

Basically the duties of active members may be summarized as follows:

1. Attend all district committee meetings.
2. Join one of the subcommittees.
3. Strive constantly to increase and improve the membership of the district committee by inviting friends and neighbors to join the district committee.
4. Prepare complaints in writing.
5. Help the police in any way possible to carry out their law enforcement duties.
6. Help make the district a safer and better place in which to live.
7. Keep a watchful eye on the neighborhood and try to correct its problems by participating fully as a citizen against crime.

8. Come to each district meeting prepared to present something that is constructive that will improve the district committee operations.

9. Never hesitate to speak at meetings, to present new ideas, to criticize where criticism is called for and to give credit where credit is due. However, avoid long, drawn-out presentations at meetings.

The citizen must remember that it is his committee and it is only as effective as he is effective. It will progress and produce good effects if he progresses and produces good work. Tht citizen, in the final analysis, will decide what kind of a neighborhood or community he will have and what kind of police force he will have.

FIRST MEETING

The first meeting of the committee will be the most important. It has to be good to generate a sufficient amount of interest. People have to know and understand what the citizen is trying to do.

The first step is to pick a meeting place that will offer wide appeal and not offend any group sensitivities. The police must select with care those who will be asked to attend that meeting. They should be leaders in their district, people who are interested in the community and the well-being of its citizens. At the meeting the police will explain the purpose and the kind of organization they are trying to establish. The police must tell the citizens that they want them to know and meet members of the police department, that they want them to know all about the police department. Primarily, they want them to know the different responsibilities. Among the things they can tell the group are the number of burglaries and car thefts, the number of major crimes, the juvenile delinquency problems, geographic areas of the special problems, and what is being done about them.

Let them understand that this is the place where they can come with their problems and get some of them off their chest. Once the police have their interest, they should become formally organized on a permanent basis.

ORGANIZATION OF POLICE-COMMUNITY RELATIONS DISTRICT COMMITTEES

Each district committee is headed by a committee chairman who, with a secretary-treasurer, vice chairman and chairman of the subcommittee, comprises the district committee. The membership of the district committee elects these officers. When the new chairman takes office, he appoints a chairman to the subcommittee. Each subcommittee chairman appoints to his subcommittee not less than five members and as many persons as volunteer.

EXECUTIVE COMMITTEE

The chairman, vice chairman, secretary-treasurer, and chairmen of the subcommittees constitute the executive committee of the district committee. The executive committee meets monthly, prior to the district committee meeting, to plan the agenda for the district committee meeting.

MEETINGS

The general membership of the district police-community relations committee will meet monthly, at a fixed time and place, preferably at the district police station. The chairman and the commander of the district conduct the meeting. The district commander or his representative is present at the meeting whenever possible and reports on the crime situation in the district. Any officers who would be of aid to the committee should be present when their services are needed. The officers often act as advisors at these meetings on problems which do not directly concern the police such as recreation or schools. If, for example, the residents wish better lighting at a certain location, the officer can use his experience to instruct the committee on the procedure to be followed to obtain the goal. At other times, the discussion might concern directly the operation of the department. Problems such as where better enforcement is needed, how better enforcement is needed, how better enforcement can be obtained, what steps the citizens can take to alleviate a particular police problem, and whether police attitudes on a particular problem are correct, may be discussed.

During these meetings the officers are able to assist the residents as well as exercise a function as the representatives of the police department. This allows the citizen to see the officers when they are not acting in a punitive role and allows the officers to observe the citizens at some time other than a confrontation in their official police duty. Through this contact, the officer and the citizen should obtain mutual understanding of each other as well as the problems which face each group in their day-to-day existence.

AGENDA. The following is a suggested agenda for fast, efficient meetings:

1. Minutes of last district committee meeting.
2. Minutes of last executive committee meeting.
3. Introduction of new members.
4. Reports of subcommittee chairman (four minutes each).
   a. Public relations committee.
   b. District committee.
   c. Executive committee.
   d. Auto theft committee.
   e. Traffic committee.
   f. Sanitation committee.
   g. Membership committee.
   h. Program committee.
5. Report on disposition of past complaints by
   a. District committee chairman.
   b. Commander of district or his representative.
6. Old business.
7. New business.
8. Complaints received.
9. Special guest speakers, when scheduled.
10. Conclusion of meeting, announcement of day, time and place of next meeting.

It is suggested that no district committee meeting last for more than one and one-half hours except when unusual business is to be conducted. Complaints should be submitted in writing so they may be processed more efficiently and effectively.

Gripes

Some of these meetings turn into "gripe" sessions. This can be painful, especially when complaints against the department are based on misinformation, half-truths and, on occasion, an obvious prejudice against policemen. There is only one thing more unpleasant than this, and that is listening to complaints that have a very good basis in fact.

In both cases, this is a necessary pain. Unless police and citizens get their mutual complaints on the table, there is no way to correct false impressions or to rectify the trouble. Needless to say, the corrective measures needed should be taken immediately either to correct the shortcoming of the department or to remove the misconception from the minds of the public.

SUBCOMMITTEES

Each district committee has eight subcommittees, these being public relations, crime, traffic, program, juvenile, sanitation, auto theft and membership. Each subcommittee must have at least five members. The continuing functions of the designated subcommittees are outlined in the ensuing paragraphs.

Public Relations Commitee

Members of this committee receive all complaints concerning the police and/or the district committee submitted by the citizens of the district, and upon investigating these complaints, submit them for appropriate action to the executive committee.

It is also the function of this committee to formulate and release, upon the approval of the district committee chairman and the police-community relations office, publicity material dealing with the operations, functions, programs and other activities of the district committee and the subcommittees of the district committee.

Crime Committee

The purpose of this committee is to review with the district commander or staff officer, the general and specific situation of crime in the district. The committee acts and proceeds in such a manner to assist the police in whatever way necessary to enhance and support police efforts in the area of crime apprehension and prevention; assist in the maintenance of law and order; develop an attitude of crime-consciousness in the community; assist the police in reducing the crime rate; support desirable and necessary police standards of the highest order; report on, and keep careful watch on, crime breeding areas in the district, and inform the citizens on what they can do to prevent, reduce, or eliminate crime. This committee meets when necessary at the request of the district committee vice chairman or the commander of the police district.

Juvenile Committee

The members of this committee receive citizen complaints of illegal or dangerous juvenile activities in the district and forward these complaints to the executive committee which then refers them to the district commander and the juvenile officer and makes a report of measures taken to resolve or meet the problem. Members of this committee receive reports on and personally observe and report on such delinquency-prone activities and areas as follows: pool rooms; loitering, corner gatherings; liquor consumption; sale of liquor to minors; violation of the curfew law; truancy; adults contributing to the delinquency of children.

The chairman of this committee shall arrange for and hold monthly meetings with his committee and the district juvenile officer to review, discuss and analyze all aspects of the juvenile problem facing the citizens and the police of the district.

Sanitation Committee

Members of this committee receive citizen's complaints of unsanitary conditions in the district. The chairman of the committee shall forward all complaints to the executive committee which will then refer them to the district commander and the district sanitation officer and report on the measures taken to correct the situation.

This committee promotes sanitary conditions and suggests ways and means of communicating with the people in the community on their responsibility toward improving and maintaining sanitary conditions.

Members of this committee receive reports on and personally observe and report on such unsanitary conditions as follows: littered streets and alleys; uncovered rubbish or garbage containers; defective sewers; unlawful burning of rubbish, and rat-infested areas.

Auto Theft Committee

Members of this committee cooperate with the police in the prevention of auto thefts and in informing the public what procedures or precautions should be employed to prevent auto theft.

Traffic Committee

Members of this committee receive citizens' complaints and suggestions from the police regarding traffic problems in the district.

Members of this committee receive reports on, or personally observe and report on, such traffic violations and problems as follows: areas of high traffic violations; abandoned autos; trucks illegally parked in residential areas; heavy trucks using restricted streets as thoroughfares; drag racing; garages where autos are being dismantled in violation of the law; inoperative electric signals; damaged stop and street signs; unrepaired surfaces of streets and alleys.

Membership Committee

This committee receives and recommends prospective members and suggests the dropping of inactive members. This committee conducts a continuing campaign to increase the membership of the committee, and should keep an accurate membership list of the committee.

Program Committee

This committee plans all programs for the district committee and assists the executive committee in preparing the agenda for committee meetings.

SPECIAL PROJECTS

In addition to the ongoing functions of each of these subcommittees, each district is permitted to select a special project it feels fulfills a serious and immediate need in the district. When initiating projects, the committee works as far as possible through existing organizations in the districts. It does not assume the functions of existing organizations or agencies that operate in the district.

While many possible projects present themselves to the committee, the police-community relations focus is kept in mind at all times. Survey, study, or educational projects are selected that bear closely on law and order, safety and other considerations not far removed from the police function.

CITY COORDINATION

In order to coordinate the activities of each of the subcommittees on the city-wide basis, an executive secretary is designated for each of the subcommittees.

The executive secretaries from like committees, such as the juvenile committees, will meet periodically under the guidance of an executive secretary who is also a chairman of the juvenile committee in his district. At these meetings they discuss their mutual needs and problems, and exchange information on a city-wide basis. In this way all activities are coordinated, duplication is eliminated, and the maximum exchange of information and assistance is assured.

ACTION PROGRAM

The key to the successful operation of any group is the involvement of the group in work on a series of clearly defined objectives, most of which are achievable and therefore a source of gratification to the group. Once the police have made their initial contacts in the neighborhood and have selected the nucleus of their citizens' groups, they must constantly provide them with action-oriented programs that will involve them in the fulfillment of the general objectives. This action-oriented program must be so diverse as to include all of the members of the group. Each member must have a clearly defined function that will occupy him continuously but not to the extent that it becomes onerous.

First, the police have the duty to set up an action program for them. Second, it will be the police's responsibility to indoctrinate them thoroughly in this program prior to its initiation. Third, it will be the responsibility of the police to see to it that the task of carrying out the program is meted out in such a way as to spread the work more or less evenly among the members. Fourth, it will be the officers' responsibility to see to it that there is a strong chairman who will carry out each phase of the program. Finally, it will be the police's responsibility to provide members with all the clerical help needed to carry out their work. Furthermore, the police will have to keep a constant check on them to see that everything functions smoothly and effectively. This demands that a staff be available at the district level on a full-time basis. Part-time amateur help needs full-time professional direction.

Police-community relation committees function as continuing entitles. During a crisis, these committees can be particularly valuable. At a time of unrest, an inflammatory rumor can spark open conflict. Because of the communication and understanding which develops through these committees, the members are able to place the rumors in proper prospective. The police then have an organized group which they can call upon, when such rumors are spreading, to inform others of the true circumstances of a situation, thereby mitigating the disquieting effects of such a rumor.

The members of a police-community relations committee can also directly assist the police during a period of tension through efforts encouraging people to stay off the streets and suggesting meaningful alternatives to violence. These members would be composed of the residents of the neighborhood, people who have an immediate interest in preserving the integrity of their area. These people would know the residents in the area and could be more persuasive than police, especially if the point of tension is police action in the particular case.

The police-community relations committee creates an atmosphere where the residents from an area are involved in the activities of the police and a police department is involved in the problems of the area. This technique provides another forum in which communication and understanding can occur.

Basically these community relations programs are an endeavor to close the gap between established law enforcement and the community it serves. The keys to success are communication and contact. However, most of all it is getting to know the people concerned and having them discuss their problems, great or small, so that solutions can be had without the antagonisms so common throughout our country today.

Chapter 13

MASS NEWS MEDIA RELATIONS

INTRODUCTION

IT IS IMPERATIVE that all news coverage be impartial, fair and complete. To accomplish this end, the police must not only maintain close and cordial relations with the press, but must supply it with full and complete information whenever this can be done. Such conduct will convince the press of the integrity and honesty of the police. Such confidence is essential in the times of stress and confusion which result from a riot. At such times the press must have complete confidence in the police, so that it can contribute to the overall effort of the police to establish and maintain order, while at the same time performing its duty to fully inform the public of the events.

IMPORTANCE OF THE NEWS MEDIA

Our free press is one of the foundations of our form of government. An outstanding difference between life in this country and life in the dictator-ruled countries is the fact that our press has the right to print whatever it chooses, subject only to the abuse of that right. The press is free to criticize any phase of government provided that all facts stated in the criticism be true. As a result, any attempt to interfere with the press or in any way to censor what it prints is a direct blow against our form of government.

The news media—press, television and radio—performs an extremely important function in our society. It supplies the public with the news, news of crime and police activity which the public has a right to know. The purpose is to help its audience to understand what is going on so that they can reach intelligent decisions about public affairs. Unfortunately, crime is one of the facts of community life, and if the public does not understand it, it is unlikely that the situation will ever be improved.

It is the responsibility of the press to keep the processes of justice under constant public scrutiny. Full news coverage of agencies of justice provide assurance against discriminatory practices or corruption in office, both on the part of enforcement officials and of the courts. It is a protection to the good official. It is an assurance against the abuses of authority by bad officials. The omnipresence of reporters and cameras has had good effects, not only in preventing police improprieties, but also in recording public evidence of prudent police action.

Crime news is an important deterrent to crime because, either directly or inferentially, it carries the warning that crime does not pay. If there is any foundation in psychology for our assumption that repetition is effective, surely the press stories of arrest, conviction and sentencing, and execution appearing day after day must make some impression on the mind of the criminally inclined. Moreover, crime news aids in the apprehension of those who have committed offenses. It permits the widest dissemination of personal descriptions. It exposes the criminal to an army of volunteer intelligence sources and forces the criminal to show his movements if he is escaping.

Crime news puts the public on guard against the perpetrator of crime, or against the perpetration of like offenses by other criminals. For many offenders crime news provides a penalty more feared than the penalties of the law. Those who would laugh off offenses or even short imprisonment, if they could pay the one or serve the other in obscurity, fear the penalties of public reproach. A short experience in dealing with those who try to keep their names out of crime news would persuade any press critic of the powerful influence upon many people of this deterrent. The confirmed criminal, the hardened law breaker, may be indifferent to this penalty, but thousands of persons who might otherwise proceed from minor to major crime are influenced by it and avoid the repetition of offenses that have led to painful publicity.

The news media throughout the nation has consistently supported such things as the following:

1. Improved criminal procedures.
2. Better police facilities.
3. Improved police management techniques.
4. Better police equipment.
5. Increases in manpower.
6. Better selection and training procedures.
7. Increased pay for police officers.
8. Improvements in moving traffic.
9. Increased traffic enforcement that shows results in terms of accident reduction.
10. Intelligent, well-conceived enforcement policies.
11. More efficient criminal court systems and speedier justice.

These are just a few items. Each jurisdiction will undoubtedly have an equally long and more specialized list that will have significant local application. The end result is that the press supports good law enforcement, and certainly these press policies could find no reasonable objection to them from professional law enforcement officers.

Certainly in the past, the news media has proved its responsibility or cooperation by voluntarily refraining from the publication of information which it knew would interfere with the successful apprehension of criminals and the rescue of kidnap victims.

In recent times, when the ill effects of certain types of coverage of riots and demonstrations were called to its attention, steps were immediately and voluntarily taken to eliminate the undesirable practices.

POLICE-PRESS RELATIONS

Good press relations have not always existed in police circles, often because of the failure of the police to appreciate the position of the press. Some have not recognized, for instance, that the news media is probably the most potent force in American life. No great public reaction, nor even a moderate expression of democratic government, is possible without the public enlightenment that flows from a free and outspoken press.

In some instances, police departments have resented the "nosiness" of the press, but even this resentment is not well founded. Newspapers live on news, and it must be timely news not cold statistics. Moreover, there is an urgency in newspaper work that requires the quoting of officers, another thing of which many policemen disapprove. Writers would be exposed to many libel suits were it not for the fact that they merely repeat what is told them by public officials. Furthermore, the public would not want to read what a newspaperman had to say about an incident since he was not in a position to know, whereas the policeman was. These are but some of the reasons reporters are sometimes unusually inquisitive about the details of a case.

Far from being a hindrance, the newspaperman often is a real asset to the police. Numerous crimes have been solved by the press receiving a "tip" and turning it over to the police. Even the recruit patrolman will admit he has been helped to overcome obstacles more than once by the seasoned and friendly newspaperman. Photographic and recording equipment possessed by the news media has been and may be made available to the police by previous agreement. Network television may make available the use of a helicopter with photographic equipment for reconnaissance purposes. Photographs and movies of the action have been made available to police for the evaluation of tactics employed or as a training media. Statements taken by reporters, but not necessarily printed, have been of value to police in planning. There is every reason to believe that in the future the police and the mass media can continue to cooperate fully; for the ultimate aim of both is the same, that is, the service to the community and attainment of justice for all.

The Press and Public Acceptance of the Police

Much of the acceptance or nonacceptance of the police by the people in the United States depends upon how the press, the radio and other mass media report or interpret the work of the police. The public will judge the adequacy and efficiency of the police department as reflected in reports of crime prevalence, police activity in crime detection and prevention, and misconduct and malfeasance on the part of the members of the force. Unfortunately, it should be recognized that normal police work is not publicized. Seldom does the public hear about the officer who carried out his assignments with a devotion to duty. This is not news. Malpractices make the headlines. Naturally, this tends to distort the image of the law enforcement officer in the thinking of the people.

Recognizing the function of the news media, and its importance in our society and to the police, is the first step toward better relations between the police and the press and, ultimately, between the police and the public. Next, a police department must have a positive goal in its press relations.

GOAL OF THE POLICE-PRESS PROGRAM

The goal of the police-press program is a maximum flow of information to the public through the press with a minimum disruption of the department's primary mission. It is impossible to lay out in detail a complete list of specifics of a press policy which would be applicable in all situations and in every organization. Each individual law enforcement organization will have unique problems which will require it to evolve its own policy of press relations. What may be a satisfactory policy in one organization would not be in another, but certain general principles can be stated. They are as follows:

1. The police must recognize that cooperation with press, motion pictures, television, radio, publishers, writers, lecturers and educators is not only desirable but is essential.

2. The police must treat all representatives of news media impartially, including the minority representatives, showing favoritism to none.

3. At the scene of a serious crime, accident, emergency or other event, permissible information, when definitely established as fact, will be promptly released. Such releases should all be made through the officer in charge or an officer designated by him.

4. Every member of the force will be respectful in his contact with others and give his name and badge number to anyone requesting it.

5. The police should not hesitate to make available to the local press newsworthy items which will tend to aid in forming a favorable public opinion of the police department. Such stories as transfers of key personnel, new recruits assigned to the division and retirements should not be overlooked as outlets. New divisional policies affecting the public, assignment of new equipment and station improvements should also be given to the press. The local press is usually interested in covering these stories in addition to crime news.

WITHHOLDING NEWS

Although full disclosure is the desired goal, there are times when limitations must be placed on news. When information is withheld, a valid reason must always exist. The action must not be arbitrary or capricious. Confessions, admissions, or other statements by the person in custody or summaries of them, should not be released to the news media by any person because of court decisions.

It must be decided what information must in certain circumstances be withheld from press representatives. Almost all police organizations have found it necessary to issue directives or regulations in this area.

There are instances where publication of all the facts of a situation may be damaging to efforts directed toward a peaceful solution. In such cases it may be necessary to ask the press to keep these facts in confidence. This request should be honored by the press. A word of caution is necessary at this point. The policy agency or individual officer who makes too great a use of "facts told in confidence" to the press media will alienate the members of the press. Most newspapermen feel it their duty to honor a confidence once it is given to them. They frequently feel, however, that the police officer who too often comes to them with circumstances or information on a confidential basis is restricting their right to the publication of the news. In extreme cases, the press sometimes refuses to accept information received in confidence realizing that if it is so accepted, the confidence must be kept, and if it is rejected, the newspapermen then have the right to find out the circumstances for themselves and print them. Thus, when a large raid or police action is planned, it is better to call the reporters and photographers to headquarters and at the proper time explain to them what is to take place, rather than have them learn of it later.

There are problem areas, such as in a kidnapping case, in the releasing of news. Here it is essential to establish relations with editors in order that they may assist if needed. A complete understanding is a must.

For many years it has been the policy of the press to treat sensational cases as a constantly unravelling "whodunit." Each move of the police is reported and future moves are disclosed. The fact that the police "have nothing to go on" has even been reported, and such statements can give aid and comfort to suspects who are being questioned by the police. Conducting criminal investigations under the glaring lamp of publicity has many obvious drawbacks, and more often than not the criminal benefits from this. This is not entirely the fault of the press because the pressure of competition makes newspapermen inclined to print anything that they can get their hands on. It is, therefore, the responsibility of the police department to write "Not for Publication" on any information which may not be used without a clearance. A definite procedure should be established for the handling of "No Publicity" cases. Those cases should be delivered to the chief in small departments and to a designated commanding officer on each shift in larger departments. Officers having information relating to them should be informed of the action taken and should refer press inquiries to the designated officer who should discuss the case with the press representatives in a group, stating the position of the department and seeking agreement with the reporters to withhold publication. When the relationships are suitable, the press representative who is unable or unwilling to refrain from publication will so notify the police, who may then discuss the matter with the city editor.

There have been repeated instances in which the press has willingly cooperated with law enforcement agencies in withholding certain information from the public. On the other hand, it must be conceded that there has been occasional irresponsibility on the part of the press that has not only increased the difficulty of the police in solving major crimes, but has even resulted in the death of innocent persons. To prevent such unfortunate events, the law enforcement agency should be prepared to resist any pressures for the release of information that it is believed would hamper an investigation if it became widely known.

ADVISORY GROUP

A public relations advisory group can do much to aid the police, not alone in the field of press relations, but in the entire field of public relations. It should be composed of high ranking individuals from the advertising, publicity and public relations fields. The group should meet regularly with key members of the department to discuss departmental problems, particularly situations involving press relations; the solutions these men offer, which are based upon their experience in their own professions, are invaluable.

PRESS OFFICER

It is beneficial to assign and train a particular officer to handle press releases and answer press inquiries. This press officer will coordinate press relations activities of the department. He will keep the public informed of new procedures and administrative changes, special problems requiring public cooperation, and police service available. He will also process requests from representatives of the press for information regarding department policy, or from writers for screen, radio, television and other agencies seeking data for special articles.

The centralization of information will simplify the work of the press, for they know with whom they are to deal, and assure a comprehensive and complete presentation of the facts rather than a fragmented and distorted conglomeration of facts and rumors. This method also prevents premature leaks, prevents favoritism and prevents contradictory or inaccurate disclosures. It also serves the police executive's requirements because he can be assured that the individual is familiar with his plans and policies.

The man who has the responsibility for dealing with the press in any police department should be chosen on the basis of his training and ability to handle the assignment. He must be loyal to the chief and to the department, and he should understand newspaper work and be able to see the problems of the reporter.

When such a position is created, there is a better chance of early identification of problem areas that arise either within the police or the press group. It is desirable that these problem areas be identified early so that the appropriate corrective action can be taken. The police can discipline their own people to secure adherence to established policy, but the press, too, must recognize that the activities of some of their representatives interfere with the accomplishment of their mutual objectives. The police executive should have a group or spokesman, representing all of the news media, with whom he can deal in resolving these problems to the end that police procedures for aiding the press to secure the news will function effectively.

RELEASE BY INDIVIDUAL OFFICER

This is a controversial point. Many police administrators would prefer to keep a tight rein on their relations with the press and will instruct individual officers that they may not release information, that the press must deal with one or two selected supervisory or command officers for their information. This policy has several drawbacks which may adversely affect police-press relations. It frequently prevents the news representatives from obtaining firsthand accounts; it prevents them from getting correct, detailed answers to all of their questions; it makes the reporter's job more difficult and may prevent him from making his deadline; and it may result in the loss of many good human interest stories because these are not always matters of official record, and the other channels of communications which might bring them to light are blocked.

Thus, even though a capable individual is responsible for the major area of press relations, he should not be the only channel of news. The newspaper representative has a requirement for securing the news today while it is still news, and he should be permitted to contact the particular officer who has the information he needs. The officer should be permitted to give the reporter the facts of the incident. However, to permit police officers to give out information to the press points out the importance of providing them with training. They should understand the desirability of cooperating with the press, and they must also be apprised of what facts should not be revealed. Information which might hamper an investigation or the identification of confidential sources of information should never be given out. The officer should also be cautioned not to divulge information about cases which are being investigated by another officer or another unit, and of which he has only cursory knowledge. Inquiries should be directed to the original sources for information.

TRAINING

The most important consideration to the administrator in making his "policy" function effectively is the training of his personnel. Although, almost without exception, all police administrators recognize the importance of maintaining good working relations with the press, this cannot be said to be true of all police officers, especially those in the lower ranks. Aside from written regulations or policies, very little effort is being expended by many organizations to improve the attitudes of their officers or to see that the policies are being fully implemented. Many techniques have been developed in various departments that deserve to receive wider recognition and use. Included among these are classroom instruction periods for recruit and in-service personnel during which areas of cooperation with the news media are clearly outlined. Seminars are held in some of the more progressive organizations which are attended by press representatives and senior police officials. These provide a useful opportunity for the discussion of mutual problems.

DEFINITE NEWS POLICY

A department should establish a definite policy on the

release of news items. There are a number of factors to be considered here. It must be remembered that news sells newspapers. Reporters want the story. They want it as soon as possible. They want to print all the news they legitimately can. Every effort should be made to assure that they receive it as quickly as possible.

There should be an established policy and a definite agreement with the newsmen relative to breaking any story of a crime that would warn suspects still at large. Almost every newspaper will voluntarily avoid such a story. The newspapers will also voluntarily avoid giving details on the specific operation of any criminal method, but the police should still have a definite understanding with them. They will be satisfied to give the general outline of the criminal method but leave out the details that would allow someone to copy any new or unusual criminal practice.

If no press officer is desigated, a definite policy must be established with regard to who will make information available to the press in given circumstances. Thus, the plan may be that information should be made public at the lowest administrative level possible. This level would be determined by the organization and size of the individual department. In a small department, the officer in charge of the blotter would receive the task of releasing information. In a larger department, certainly, the unit heads or division commanders should be given this authority. Press conferences called by the chief or one of his assistants might be necessary on occasions but the press should have direct access to the men in charge of the department at any given time.

In an emergency situation important enough to bring out a senior officer of the department to take charge, certainly releases should be made through him. This serves two purposes; first, it tends to cut down rumors, and second, it permits the dissemination of news to all reporters at the same time.

USE OF INDIVIDUAL POLICEMAN'S NAME

The use of the names of individual police officers in news stories is a controversial point. The press will frequently insist that this practice enhances the value of its story. From the police department's point of view, it is probably a more favorable rule to request that the names of individual personnel not be used in the vast majority of cases. Unusually heroic actions or effective police work may occasionally warrant the use of the officer's name; but by avoiding the use of officers' names, a large number of minor internal problems can be avoided. No department is without its "headline-happy" individuals and not infrequently these personnel provide the so-called internal leaks to the press on many subjects about which they are not fully informed. The occasional resentments that grow up between the personnel of divisions is frequently predicated on the one receiving credit for a particularly important arrest that may have actually been effected by personnel of the other division.

COORDINATION

One of the important areas that must receive great attention in planning any press program is that of coordination between the various law enforcement agencies and the office of public prosecution, regarding what information may be released or printed. Lack of coordination will result in embarrassment and even strained relations between these cooperating governmental units. Frictions between police departments in investigations which are being cooperatively pursued are not an uncommon occurrence and frequently have arisen as a result of this problem. This can be avoided if, in advance, a definite procedure for handling press releases has been established.

It should be standard procedure that if another department or agency is concerned, a superior of that agency should be consulted before discussing a phase of the incident involving that agency.

GENERAL RULES FOR BETTER RELATIONS

There are general rules that will aid greatly in bettering relations between the police and the press, for it is not sufficient for the two merely to "understand" each other. There must be sound, workable policies which, when effectively carried out, reduce the areas of conflict to livable dimensions.

1. Clearly define policies regarding dissemination of information. Determine whether the department will make centralized or decentralized release of information. If a combination of the two methods is to be used, firm up workable guidelines. Once established, maintain these policies.

2. Hold regular conferences with news officials conferences—preferably informal—should be held with the highest ranking members of the news media—editors, news directors, publishers. Schedule separate conferences for personnel in radio, television and newspapers. Discuss with them policy decisions and major departmental changes that will affect them. Make known the impartial position of the police and their determination to perform their duty to protect society by a strict, impartial enforcement of the law. Let them know you will be cooperative and helpful toward the press, and that you have made definite provision for giving accurate information to this agency of public opinion. Following the conference, inform all of the regular reporters you deal with locally of the results.

3. Hold regular conferences with working members of the press. In addition to conferences held with high ranking members of the press, conferences with the "working press" will give you an opportunity to discuss any recent developments or issues, or other information of interest to the community. Again, the keynote is a working rapport.

4. Do not take "detrimental coverage" for granted. By establishing rapport with the press, you are in a substantially better position to ask its cooperation in dealing with matters which would detrimentally affect the law enforcement image in the mind of the public. When an explanation is made of the reason why a release may not be in the public interest, the news media, as a result of this frankness, is usually quite eager to cooperate.

5. Plan the release of information. Care should be exercised in stating opinions either as to cause, extent, result, effect, duration, suspects, or similar speculation. Information with immediate news value should be released immediately.

The existence of a competitive press situation is an important consideration for the administrator. Competing newspapers are jealous of their rights and resent any evidence of news being withheld from release until after their deadline. Police management must insure the release of news as cases are reported and as soon as investigative information is available, and they should scrutinize their press operations carefully for any evidence of news favoritism on the part of the members of their organization. However, releases of general information, such as police statements, annual reports and crime statistics, should be planned so that all news agencies will have an equal time advantage (i.e., some for release in the morning, some for release in the afternoon, consider deadlines, etc.).

When you complete a major report of news value, such as your departmental annual report, make the press aware of it by, first, preparing a fact sheet with information on what the report contains, and second, giving the fact sheet to the press before the report is released. Let them know when they will be permitted to use the report. You will find that your request will be honored, and that you have created interest in your presentation.

6. Ignore occasional press criticism. Consider the overall picture, rather than a single incident. Do not let your reaction be one of animosity or antagonism; if your press relations are generally good, then let that be your guideline.

7. Take steps within your own department to avoid news leaks by letting your personnel know what is expected of them. Indoctrinate them in the preparation of news releases and procedures for the release of information. Playing favorites in this regard is dangerous indeed!

If the leak was accidental, contact the news service and let them know the circumstances; then take steps to make certain it does not recur. If it was deliberate, disciplinary action is in order.

8. Present your side of the case. From time to time we are all criticized by the press for our actions in a particular situation. When this happens to you, do not just remain idle and do nothing to protect your department. Ask your news service for an opportunity to present your side of the story, as a public service. You can gain a tremendous amount of support by

doing this, as well as let the press know that, when unjustly criticized, you are going to do whatever you can to invalidate that criticism.

9. Reports, whether a police report or a press release, should be presented in a style and language that is usable and understandable by the press. This type of preparation is in the best interests of all persons concerned with police cases, except when highly technical data must be included; even then, clarity and simplicity are of great importance.

10. Written press releases should be prepared on such subjects as policy statements and crime statistics. On the other hand, news stories should be telephoned to the press; tell them the facts, and let them write their own story.

11. Treat the newsmen with respect; they will treat you the same way. This is one of the first steps in creating and maintaining good rapport, and it is up to us to start a movement in this direction. In many areas, it is long overdue.

12. Police records must be defined as to which are available to the public, and these should be easily reached by the reporter. Specific policies must be devised to handle releases on certain crimes, photographing of prisoners and suspects, etc. Of course, these rules can only apply inside the police building. Whether or not reporters should interview prisoners is still an unresolved question. If mug shots are provided in some cases, they should be provided in all cases.

13. Minority news media should be treated the same as all others. The police officer should have the same helpful attitude toward representatives of the minority-group press as he has toward members of the majority-group press.

The minority press depends for its existence largely on the fact that each paper reports matters about, and of interest to, members of its own minority which are treated only briefly or omitted in most metropolitan newspapers. A great many minority newspapers also depend on protest stories and sensationalism for their circulation. A favorite target of such papers is the police force. By establishing a solid liaison with the minority press, the police force can do a great deal to influence those papers to publish stories that reflect credit on the police

force. Such stories in minority newspapers would have a tremendous effect in improving the public relations of the police
with that minority group.

It is therefore important that the police familiarize themselves
with the minority press in their community. A person-to-person
acquaintanceship with the editors and publishers of these organs
will go a long way toward providing sources of intelligence for
law enforcement officials, and afford a means whereby news
regarding incidents involving minority peoples will be handled
by the press in a fair and dispassionate manner. This reciprocity
is ensured where the minority press has experience and reason
to believe that the police are treating all classes and groups
with strict impartiality. The constructive influence of the minority press in obtaining and maintaining respect for the law and
cooperation with law enforcement officers should not be underestimated.

14. Every police officer observes a number of unusual or interesting items that would make good newspaper stories. Anything that is unusual, particularly if it relates to animals,
children or other elements of human interest is of importance
to the newspaper. These should be passed on to the press.

15. A cardinal rule is "Don't get publicity happy!" There
are policemen who call up the newspaper every time anything
the least bit unusual happens. They make every effort to get
their name or picture in the paper, and as a result they are not
liked either by their fellow officers or by the reporters.

16. Do not try to get the press to withhold news. Never
expect a newspaper to withhold any facts because you or any
city official or prominent citizen want the facts to be withheld.
If a newspaper is any good at all and if it is to be trusted
as a news medium, it will not withhold the facts relative to
anyone you arrest except in certain definite instances. No matter
how much a prominent citizen wants to conceal the fact that
he was arrested in the company of a woman not his wife, the
newspapers will still print the story if it is news.

Duty of the Press

A discussion of rights and duties would be incomplete

without reference to those of the press. There is a responsibility, even a moral obligation, for news media to be objective in reporting.

The handling of crime news is an area in which the press must demonstrate a greater sense of public responsibility. There have been cases where situations have been presented to the public out of all proper proportions to actual conditions. If a misquote appears or if a story or news item is slanted to reflect unfavorably upon the police agency, immediate steps should be taken to correct the matter.

Discourage Sensationalism

The police have a responsibility to call to the attention of the press the damaging effect upon community relations of the use of senationalism, particularly in relation to racial conflict. Inflammatory statements and photographs and confusing reports only tend to aggravate the situation. News accounts deliberately slanted or overstated in one direction or another only work at cross purposes to the objectives of every person involved.

The function of the press is to observe and report what happens in situations of racial tension and violence. It is not the function of the press to participate in or to influence the events. Occasionally, press representatives have hired members of each race to stage demonstrations so that pictures might be taken. This tended to inflame passions that were already aroused and fostered the kind of atmosphere necessary for the spread of rumors.

If the police are to maintain the peace, they cannot allow such practices to exist. Ultimately, they are at odds with the best interests and the peace of the areas directly involved, as well as the country as a whole. In the past, when the disastrous community consequences of such a policy have been called to the attention of the press, it has demonstrated its genuine public interest by voluntarily cooperating fully. There is every reason to believe it will demonstrate the same responsible attitude in the future.

Irresponsible Reporters

In the unusual event that a photographer or reporter proves that his primary interest is in sensationalism and makes attempts to foment actual physical violence so that he may report it, the police should take decisive action. Such action will always be condoned, and even applauded, by the responsible news-gathering agencies. Further, these cases should be promptly reported to the management of the media concerned. Those persons who have the responsibility for establishing the policy of a press media are normally far removed from the field. They are sometimes not in a position to know of the activities of their individual representatives. Frequently, the only way they have of knowing that their representatives are furnishing mis-leading but highly newsworthy material is from a contact by police officials. The foregoing comments are not made to indi-cate a failure on the part of representatives of news media to cooperate with the police, for such is not the case.

Police officers have a legitimate objection to the Machia-vellian practices of news reporters who operate on the principal that "the end justifies the means." It is not infrequent to find reporters, pressed by their deadlines, resorting to practices which seriously impede police investigations. Among these is the tendency to make telephone calls to addresses at which serious crimes have been reported and, representing themselves as senior police officials, begin questioning the occupants. These and many other news practices should have been discarded long ago but, alas, they are still all too prevalent in the larger cities. When these incidents occur, the police administrator should act immediately to make his position clear with the editors of the papers involved and should request that these particular rep-resentatives be removed from the police beat.

PRESS PASSES

A number of police organizations have adopted the practice of issuing standard identification credentials to full-time mem-bers of the working press with the understanding that such credentials may be used in passing police lines in areas where these have been established. The privileges granted by such documents vary widely from one jurisdiction to another, and admittedly such documents could conceivably be a source of possible abuse. But the vast majority of the press representatives will not abuse privileges granted thereby, and much good could be derived from this practice.

FREE-LANCE PRESS

A separate policy should be adopted with respect to free-lance journalists and photographers. These individuals usually are citizens who own cameras and their objective is to secure pictures which may have some commercial value. Persons lacking proper press credentials should be excluded from a closed area when police lines have been erected.

PERIOD OF TENSION

In a period of tension reporters should be made acquainted with the department's general policy for dealing with public disorders. This will aid greatly in avoiding misinterpretation of events that may occur in the course of an actual outbreak.

It is important that the press be enlisted in campaigns to dispel rumors and establish the facts. The only antidote for poisonous rumor is fact. It is axiomatic that the wider the facts of a situation are circulated, the greater difficulty rumor will have in finding a following. Because of this necessary communication of facts, the press, by which we mean newspaper, television and radio news gatherers is of great importance in controlling the spread of rumor.

In periods of tension it is important that the press be actively solicited to assist in campaigns calculated to dispel rumor and establish fact. A frank approach is in most cases the best policy, for if the press begins to doubt police versions of the circumstances of a particular situation, it may not act readily enough in killing rumors.

The intelligent use of news media and other devices available to the police is an important adjunct to the preventive effort. Neighborhood news bulletins and leaflets in English or foreign languages may be used to distribute information important to the issue being disputed. These devices help provide information that will control the emotions of persons involved in a dispute. Once a crowd or mob has been formed, the use of informational devices must be continued in an effort to control the group and prevent violence.

The police must also make every effort to provide security to news plants, television and radio stations if there is any possibility of mob violence or destruction to such installations. Any mob action which has a semblance of organization may intend to damage news media installations to prevent publication of factual information. Cooperative relationships with civic and minority group organizations are of great value in checking the flow of rumors.

RELATIONS AT TIME OF RIOT OR DISASTER

A system of accrediting newsmen must be established in advance of trouble and special laminated ID cards issued periodically. Only those press representatives who are so accredited should be allowed in the otherwise isolated riot area.

Full cooperation and protection should be afforded all newsmen in the riot area. They shoudl be advised of the danger centers, but so long as they do not interfere with the tactical operations of the police, it is up to them to make the decision whether or not they will enter such areas.

A public information officer should be provided by the law enforcement agency to deal directly with the press concerning the riot situation. The public information officer should deal with the news agencies, local papers, radio, and television stations to cope with rumors and to enlist their cooperation in playing down emotional news coverage which incites and inflames the public. A special press room may be set up at the agency's headquarters for the press to be briefed on developments. An understanding should be reached concerning the use of camera crews and reporters at the scene of the riot. *For a more detailed treatment of press problems and procedure see Riots, Revolts and Insurrections.*

INDEX